delish

— INSANELY EASY —
CASSEROLES

80+
AMAZING
COMFORT FOOD
RECIPES

© 2020 by Hearst Magazines, Inc.

Photographs by Parker Feierbach, Ethan Calabrese,
Kat Wirsing, and Beatriz De Costa
Book design by Christy Sabido

Library of Congress Cataloging–in–Publication Data
is on file with the publisher.

978–1–950099–63–4
4 6 8 10 9 7 5 3 paperback

HEARST

CASSEROLES
HAVE ALWAYS AND WILL ALWAYS BE COOL

When you're feeding a crowd, you reach for your 9x13-inch pan. Be it Classic Baked Ziti (p. 84), Philly Cheesesteak Casserole (p. 49), Chicken Spinach Artichoke Bake (p. 27), or Loaded Cauli "Mac" (p. 97), casseroles are cozy comfort foods that'll never let you or your guests down. They may not always be the sexiest (Turkey Tettrazini, p. 80, we still 🖤 you), but they'll always be devoured.

In this book, you'll find old-school classics, new favorites, and, yes, even desserts. No, nobody considers a poke cake a casserole. But the same pan that made your Cheesy Bacon-Asparagus Casserole (p. 117) can also make Death by Chocolate Poke Cake (p. 155), and that's pretty incredible.

Plus, what exactly is a casserole anyway? Thousands of people google that very question each and every month because NOBODY KNOWS. And to be honest, we don't really care. What's important to us is that whether you're throwing a party, hosting overnight guests, celebrating a birthday, or making Tuesday night's dinner, you'll find the perfect, most delicious recipes in this book.

XO,
Team Delish

CONTENTS

CHAPTER 7

AMAZING DESSERTS

CHAPTER 5

HEALTHY COMFORT FOOD

CHAPTER 8

BRUNCH FAVORITES

CHAPTER 6

BEST-EVER SIDES

CHAPTER

1

APPS & BITES

PULL-APART GARLIC BREAD PIZZA DIP

TOTAL TIME
1 HR 15 MIN

SERVES 8

This recipe has been tested upward of 10 times, and not one person on the team ever complained about it. Were we trying to make it absolutely perfect? Yes. Were we also always trying to think of an excuse to eat it? Yes.

---

3 cups shredded mozzarella, divided

2 (8-ounce) blocks cream cheese, softened

1 cup ricotta

⅓ cup plus 2 tablespoons freshly grated Parmesan, divided

1 tablespoon Italian seasoning

½ teaspoon crushed red pepper flakes

Kosher salt

¾ cup pizza sauce

1 cup mini pepperoni

2 (16-ounce) cans refrigerated biscuits (such as Pillsbury Grands)

¼ cup extra-virgin olive oil

3 cloves garlic, minced

1 tablespoon freshly chopped parsley

---

1. Preheat oven to 350°. In a large bowl, mix together 2 cups mozzarella, cream cheese, ricotta, ⅓ cup Parmesan, Italian seasoning, and red pepper flakes and season with salt. Transfer mixture to a 9x13-inch baking dish and spread pizza sauce over it. Top with remaining 1 cup mozzarella and pepperoni.

2. Halve biscuits and roll into balls, then place on top of dip.

3. In a small bowl, whisk together oil, garlic, and parsley. Brush on biscuits and sprinkle with remaining 2 tablespoons Parmesan.

4. Bake until biscuits are golden and cheese is melty, about 45 minutes, then cover and bake until biscuits are cooked through, another 15 to 20 minutes.

5. Let cool 10 minutes before serving.

PRO TIP!
Use the scooped-out potatoes to make a potato soup, or fry them into mashed potato balls!

CHEESESTEAK POTATO SKINS

TOTAL TIME
1 HR 15 MIN

MAKES 8

If you thought loaded potato skins couldn't get any better, you'd be very wrong. Filling them with seared steak, sautéed peppers and onions, and melty provolone is unbeatable.

6 russet potatoes, scrubbed clean
3 tablespoons extra–virgin olive oil, divided
Kosher salt

Freshly ground black pepper
1 large onion, thinly sliced
2 bell peppers, thinly sliced
1½ pounds flank steak, thinly sliced

1 teaspoon dried oregano
⅔ cup shredded provolone
1 tablespoon freshly chopped parsley, for garnish

1. Preheat oven to 400°. Pierce potatoes all over with a fork, then rub with 2 tablespoons oil and season with salt and pepper. Place potatoes in a large baking dish and bake until skin is crispy and potatoes are tender, about 1 hour. Let cool slightly until cool enough to handle.

2. Meanwhile, make filling: In a large skillet over medium heat, heat remaining 1 tablespoon oil. Add onion and peppers and cook until soft, 5 minutes. Add steak and season with oregano, salt, and pepper. Cook until steak is cooked through, 5 minutes for medium.

3. When potatoes are cool enough to handle, cut them in half lengthwise. Scoop out flesh with a spoon, leaving a ¼–inch border. (Reserve scooped–out middles for a different use.) Return potatoes, cut–side up, to baking dish. Divide steak mixture evenly among potatoes then top with provolone.

4. Bake until cheese is melty, 10 minutes.

5. Garnish with parsley before serving.

ANTIPASTO SQUARES

TOTAL TIME
1 HR

SERVES
6

True, there's nothing that *wouldn't* taste delicious sandwiched between two sheets of crescent rolls. But the combination you're working with here is truly transcendent.

Cooking spray
2 (8–ounce) tubes crescent rolls, divided
½ pound deli ham
¼ pound pepperoni

½ pound sliced provolone
¼ pound sliced mozzarella
1 (16–ounce) jar sliced pepperoncini, drained

2 tablespoons extra-virgin olive oil
¼ cup freshly grated Parmesan
1 teaspoon dried oregano

---

1. Preheat oven to 350° and grease a 9x13–inch baking dish with cooking spray.

2. Unroll one tube of crescents in prepared baking dish and pinch together seams. Layer ham, pepperoni, provolone, mozzarella, and pepperoncini.

3. Unroll remaining tube of crescent dough and place on top of pepperoncini. Pinch together seams to seal, then brush all over with oil. Sprinkle with Parmesan and oregano.

4. Bake until dough is golden and cooked through, about 35 minutes. (If dough is browning too quickly, cover with foil.)

5. Let cool at least 15 minutes before slicing into squares.

HAM & CHEESE SLIDERS

TOTAL TIME
25 MIN

SERVES
12

Put down the Dijon mustard. Yellow mustard's bright acidic flavor is perfect for this homemade poppy seed dressing. (But if you only have Dijon, ugh, that's fine too.)

¼ cup mustard

1 tablespoon honey

4 tablespoons melted butter

1 tablespoon poppy seeds

12 slider buns

¼ cup mayonnaise

12 slices deli ham

12 slices Swiss cheese

---

1. Heat oven to 350° and line a large baking sheet with parchment paper.

2. In a small bowl, whisk together the mustard and honey.

3. Make poppy seed dressing: In a medium bowl, whisk together the butter, poppy seeds, and 1 tablespoon of honey–mustard mixture.

4. Split slider buns in half horizontally and place bottom half on baking sheet. Spread mayo in an even layer on the bottom layer of slider buns, then top with an even layer of ham and cheese. Spread cut side of top buns with honey–mustard mixture then place on top of cheese layer. Pour poppy seed dressing on tops of buns (using a pastry brush to spread if necessary) until all buns are coated.

5. Place in oven and bake until cheese is melty and buns are golden, 10 to 12 minutes. Slice before serving.

PERFECT STUFFED MUSHROOMS

TOTAL TIME
35 MIN

MAKES
6

Everyone should know how to make old-school stuffed mushrooms. They're classy but not fussy, and once you have this basic recipe down, you can go a little crazy with the filling.

Cooking spray

1½ pounds baby mushrooms, stems removed and roughly chopped

2 tablespoons butter

2 cloves garlic, minced

¼ cup bread crumbs

Kosher salt

Freshly ground black pepper

¼ cup freshly grated Parmesan, plus more for topping

4 ounces cream cheese, softened

2 tablespoons freshly chopped parsley

1 tablespoon freshly chopped thyme

1. Preheat oven to 400° and grease a large baking dish with cooking spray.

2. Place mushroom caps in prepared baking dish, stem-side up.

3. In a medium skillet over medium heat, melt butter. Add chopped mushroom stems and cook until most of the moisture is released, 5 minutes.

4. Add garlic and cook until fragrant, 1 minute, then add bread crumbs and toast lightly, 3 minutes. Season with salt and pepper. Remove from heat and let cool slightly.

5. In a large bowl, combine mushroom stem mixture, Parmesan, cream cheese, parsley, and thyme. Season with salt and pepper.

6. Fill mushroom caps with filling and sprinkle with additional Parmesan.

7. Bake until mushrooms are tender and tops are golden, 20 minutes.

MIX IT UP!
This cream cheese filling tastes amazing when mixed with chopped bacon, crumbled Italian sausage, or crab meat.

PRO TIP!

Be sure to roll these extra tight to get those mesmerizing spirals.

FRENCH DIP PINWHEELS

TOTAL TIME **1** HR **15** MIN

MAKES **10**

No matter the party—be it the Super Bowl, holiday, book club, or baby shower—these pinwheels are guaranteed to disappear first.

FOR THE PINWHEELS
Cooking spray
2 tablespoons butter
2 large onions, thinly sliced
2 sprigs fresh thyme
Kosher salt
Freshly ground black pepper
All-purpose flour, for surface
2 (8-ounce) cans crescent
 roll dough

8 slices provolone
½ pound deli roast beef
2 teaspoons fresh thyme
 leaves

FOR THE AU JUS
1 tablespoon butter
1 clove garlic, minced
1½ cups low-sodium
 beef broth

1 tablespoon Worcestershire
 sauce
¼ teaspoon fresh thyme
 leaves
Kosher salt
Freshly ground black pepper

---

1. Preheat oven to 350° and grease a 9x13-inch baking pan with cooking spray.

2. In a large skillet over medium-high heat, melt butter. Add onion and thyme sprigs and cook, stirring occasionally, until onions begin to soften and turn golden, about 5 minutes. Season with salt and pepper and reduce heat to medium. Continue cooking, stirring occasionally, until onions are soft and caramelized, 10 to 15 minutes more.

3. Assemble pinwheels: On a lightly floured surface, unroll both tubes of crescent dough and separate each into four rectangles. Pinch together seams. Top each rectangle with provolone, roast beef, and caramelized onions.

4. Starting with the short side, roll up each rectangle. Pinch edges to seal, then cut each roll into 4 slices and place cut-side up in baking dish. Sprinkle with thyme leaves.

5. Bake until dough is golden, 35 minutes.

6. Meanwhile, make au jus: In a small saucepan over medium heat, melt butter. Stir in garlic and cook until fragrant, about 1 minute. Add broth, Worcestershire, and thyme leaves and season with salt and pepper. Simmer until slightly reduced, 10 minutes.

7. Serve pinwheels warm with au jus for dipping.

BEEF TOTCHOS

TOTAL TIME 50 MIN

SERVES 8

Everyone loves tater tots. Everyone loves nachos. Everyone will love totchos. It's basic math.

Cooking spray
2 (1–pound) bags frozen tater tots
1 pound ground beef
1 tablespoon taco seasoning

1 cup cherry tomatoes, quartered
1 cup black beans
1 jalapeño, sliced
1 cup shredded cheddar

1 cup shredded Monterey jack
Sour cream, for serving
Guacamole, for serving
Freshly chopped cilantro, for serving

1. Preheat oven to 450° and grease a 9x13–inch baking dish with cooking spray.

2. Add tater tots and bake until crispy, 20 minutes.

3. In a large skillet over medium heat, heat oil. Add beef and cook until no longer pink, 6 minutes. Drain fat.

4. Return skillet to stove and season beef with taco seasoning.

5. Top tater tots with beef, tomatoes, black beans, jalapeños, and cheeses.

6. Bake until warmed through and cheese is melty, 10 minutes.

7. Top with sour cream, guacamole, and cilantro before serving.

CHAPTER
2

CHICKEN
DINNERS

HARVEST CHICKEN CASSEROLE

TOTAL TIME
1 HR 20 MIN

SERVES **8**

Packed with good-for-you ingredients, this hearty casserole is a meal prep dream.

---

2 tablespoons extra-virgin olive oil, divided, plus more for baking dish

2 pounds boneless skinless chicken breasts

Kosher salt

Freshly ground black pepper

½ onion, chopped

2 medium sweet potatoes, peeled and cut into small cubes

1 pound Brussels sprouts, trimmed and quartered

2 cloves garlic, minced

2 teaspoons fresh thyme leaves

1 teaspoon paprika

½ teaspoon ground cumin

½ cup low-sodium chicken broth, divided

6 cups cooked wild rice

½ cup dried cranberries

½ cup sliced almonds

---

1. Preheat oven to 350° and grease a 9x13-inch baking dish with oil.

2. In a large, deep skillet over medium-high heat, heat 1 tablespoon oil. Season chicken with salt and pepper then add to skillet and cook until golden and cooked through, 8 minutes per side. Let rest 10 minutes before cutting into 1-inch pieces.

3. Heat another tablespoon oil over medium heat. Add onion, sweet potatoes, Brussels sprouts, garlic, thyme, paprika, and cumin. Season with salt and pepper and cook until softened, 5 minutes. Add ¼ cup broth, bring to a simmer, and cook, covered, 5 minutes.

4. Place cooked rice in a large baking dish and season with salt and pepper. Stir in chicken, cranberries, cooked vegetables, and remaining ¼ cup broth. Top with almonds and bake until dish is hot and almonds are toasted, 15 to 18 minutes.

CHICKEN SPINACH ARTICHOKE BAKE

TOTAL TIME
45 MIN

SERVES
6

When you're obsessed with spinach artichoke dip but can't justify eating it for dinner, this cheesy rice bake is how you convince yourself.

¾ cup basmati rice

1½ cups whole milk

½ cup freshly grated Parmesan

6 ounces cream cheese, cubed

2 cloves garlic, minced

Crushed red pepper flakes

Kosher salt

Freshly ground black pepper

4 cups cooked shredded chicken

2 cups packed fresh spinach

1 (14-ounce) can artichoke hearts, drained and quartered

2 cups shredded mozzarella, divided

---

1. Preheat oven to 350°. Prepare rice according to package instructions.

2. In a medium saucepan over medium heat, combine milk, Parmesan, cream cheese, garlic, and red pepper flakes and season with salt and pepper. Cook until cheeses have melted and mixture is slightly thickened, about 4 minutes.

3. In a large bowl, stir together cooked rice, chicken, spinach, artichoke hearts, 1 cup mozzarella, and cream cheese mixture and transfer to a 9x13–inch baking dish.

4. Top with remaining 1 cup mozzarella and bake until cheese is melty and golden, 20 minutes.

MAPLE MUSTARD CHICKEN LEGS

TOTAL TIME
45 MIN

SERVES 4–6

This dish has the same effect as a whole roasted bird (i.e., you'll look like a pro if you serve it to friends) but takes about half the time.

¾ pound baby potatoes, halved

½ pound small carrots, halved

2 tablespoons extra-virgin olive oil, divided

Kosher salt

Freshly ground black pepper

4 pounds whole chicken legs with thighs attached, room temperature

2 tablespoons Dijon mustard

2 tablespoons whole-grain mustard

1 tablespoon maple syrup

1 teaspoon fresh thyme leaves

Pinch crushed red pepper flakes

Freshly chopped parsley, for garnish

1. Preheat oven to 450°. In bottom of a large baking dish, toss potatoes and carrots with 1 tablespoon oil. Season with salt and pepper.

2. Pat chicken dry with paper towels, drizzle with remaining tablespoon oil, and season with salt and pepper. Arrange, skin-side up, on top of vegetables in baking dish.

3. In a small bowl, stir together mustards, maple syrup, thyme, and red pepper flakes. Brush on top of chicken and drizzle any extra over vegetables. Roast chicken until skin is golden and chicken is cooked through, about 30 minutes.

4. Heat broiler. Brush chicken with sauce collected on the bottom of the dish then broil until deeply golden, about 2 to 3 minutes.

5. Garnish with parsley before serving.

PRO TIP!
The maple mustard mixture is also amazing on salmon! Spread it on salmon fillets before baking.

CHICKEN & RICE CASSEROLE

TOTAL TIME
1 HR
40 MIN

MAKES
3

When we say anyone can cook this creamy rice casserole, we really mean *anyone*. You quite literally dump everything into one dish and wait while the oven does the rest. (Waiting is the hardest part!)

Extra-virgin olive oil, for baking dish

2 cups white rice, rinsed well and drained

1 large onion, chopped

2 cups low-sodium chicken broth

2 (10.5-ounce) cans cream of mushroom soup

Kosher salt

Freshly ground black pepper

3 large bone-in, skin-on chicken thighs

2 tablespoons melted butter

2 teaspoons fresh thyme

1 clove garlic, finely minced

1 tablespoon freshly chopped parsley, for garnish

---

1. Preheat oven to 350° and grease a 9x13-inch baking dish with oil.

2. Add rice, onion, broth, and soup and stir until combined. Season with salt and pepper.

3. Place chicken thighs in rice mixture and brush with melted butter. Sprinkle with thyme and garlic and season with salt and pepper.

4. Cover dish with foil and bake for 1 hour. Uncover and cook until rice is done and chicken is cooked through, 30 minutes more. Turn oven to broil and broil until chicken is golden, 3 to 5 minutes.

5. Garnish with parsley before serving.

CHICKEN BAKED TACOS

TOTAL TIME
30 MIN

SERVES 4-6

Tacos can be tricky to serve warm all at once, but we figured out how to cook TWELVE at a time. Consider Taco Tuesday changed forever.

---

1 tablespoon vegetable oil
1 onion, chopped
1 tablespoon ground cumin
Kosher salt
Freshly ground black pepper

3 cups shredded chicken
1 cup salsa
1 (4.5-ounce) can green chiles
1 (16-ounce) can refried beans

12 hard taco shells
1½ cups shredded pepper jack
Freshly chopped cilantro, for garnish

---

1. Preheat oven to 375°. In a large skillet over medium heat, heat oil. Add onion and cook until soft, 5 minutes, then add cumin and season with salt and pepper. Stir in chicken, salsa, and chiles.

2. Spoon refried beans into bottom of a taco shell and top with chicken mixture. Place in a 9x13-inch baking dish. Repeat, tightly standing up tacos in dish.

3. Sprinkle with cheese and bake until melty, 10 minutes. Garnish with cilantro before serving.

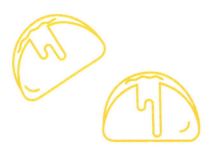

PRO TIP!

Don't have buttermilk? Whisk ¾ teaspoon lemon juice into whole milk and let sit 10 minutes before using.

BAKED CHICKEN PARM

TOTAL TIME

45 MIN

SERVES
4

Real talk: Frying chicken cutlets is a messy and unhealthy endeavor. Cut back on the hands–on time and the calories by baking the chicken instead.

¾ cup bread crumbs

¼ cup freshly grated
   Parmesan, plus more
   for garnish

1 teaspoon garlic powder

1 teaspoon Italian seasoning

2 large eggs

¼ cup buttermilk

4 boneless skinless chicken
   breasts

Kosher salt

Freshly ground black pepper

1 (32–ounce) jar marinara

1 cup shredded fresh
   mozzarella

¼ cup freshly sliced basil

---

1. Preheat oven to 400°. In a medium bowl, mix together bread crumbs, Parmesan, garlic powder, and Italian seasoning.

2. In another medium bowl, whisk together eggs and buttermilk. Pat chicken breasts dry and season both sides with salt and pepper. Dip into egg mixture, then dredge in bread crumb mixture, making sure all sides are coated.

3. Place in a large baking baking dish and bake until golden and crispy, 20 minutes.

4. Pour marinara over center of chicken breasts and top with mozzarella. Pour remaining marinara around chicken. Bake until chicken is cooked through, 10 to 15 minutes more.

5. Garnish with Parmesan and basil before serving.

CHICKEN ENCHILADA CASSEROLE

TOTAL TIME
50 MIN

SERVES 10

With layers of tortillas, enchilada sauce, and chicken, you're essentially dealing with a Tex-Mex lasagna. And it's glorious.

2 tablespoons extra-virgin olive oil
1 medium onion, chopped
1 bell pepper, chopped
2 cloves garlic, minced
3 cups cooked shredded chicken

1 (15.5-ounce) can black beans, drained and rinsed
1 (15.25-ounce) can corn, drained
1 (4.5-ounce) can diced green chiles
2 (10-ounce) cans enchilada sauce

18 small corn tortillas
2 cups shredded cheddar
2 cups shredded Monterey jack
Sour cream, for garnish
Fresh cilantro, for garnish
Diced avocado, for garnish

1. Preheat oven to 350°. In a large skillet over medium heat, heat oil. Add onion and bell pepper and cook until soft, 5 minutes. Add garlic and cook until fragrant, 1 minute more. Add chicken, beans, corn, and chiles and cook until warmed through, 5 minutes. Reserve ½ cup enchilada sauce, then pour remaining sauce into skillet, stirring to combine.

2. Spread reserved enchilada sauce on bottom of a 9x13-inch baking dish, then lay down 6 tortillas, overlapping them slightly. Pour one-third of chicken mixture over tortillas and top with about one-third of each cheese. Top with another layer of tortillas and repeat to make 2 more layers, finishing with cheese.

3. Bake until cheese is melty and sauce is bubbly, 30 minutes.

4. Garnish with sour cream, cilantro, and avocado before serving.

GREEK STUFFED CHICKEN

TOTAL TIME
45 MIN

SERVES
4

How to make chicken breasts not boring: stuff the hell out of them. Zucchini, tomatoes, lemons, and feta add a fresh Mediterranean vibe you'll love.

4 boneless skinless chicken breasts

3 tablespoons extra-virgin olive oil

1 tablespoon lemon juice

1 tablespoon freshly chopped dill, plus more for garnish

1 tablespoon freshly chopped parsley, plus more for garnish

2 cloves garlic, minced

Kosher salt

Freshly ground black pepper

1 zucchini, thinly sliced into half moons

2 medium tomatoes, thinly sliced into half moons

½ small red onion, thinly sliced into half moons

2 lemons, thinly sliced into half moons

1 cup crumbled feta

1 cup shredded mozzarella

1. Preheat oven to 400°. Make slits in each chicken breast, being careful not to cut through completely. Transfer to a large baking baking dish.

2. In a small bowl, whisk together oil, lemon juice, dill, parsley, and garlic. Drizzle over chicken, making sure oil mixture gets into the slits. Season with salt and pepper.

3. Stuff each chicken breast with zucchini, tomatoes, red onion, and lemons. Sprinkle with crumbled feta and mozzarella.

4. Bake until chicken is cooked through and no longer pink, about 25 minutes.

5. Garnish with dill and parsley before serving.

CLASSIC ROAST CHICKEN

TOTAL TIME
1 HR 30 MIN

SERVES
6

Situations for which you should roast a chicken: It's someone's birthday. Your in–laws are coming over. You're feeling the winter blues. You're celebrating a promotion. It's Sunday night.

---

1 (3½–pound) chicken
Kosher salt
Freshly ground black pepper
1 yellow onion, cut into
    large pieces

3 medium carrots, peeled and
    cut into large pieces
2 stalks celery, cut into large
    pieces
½ pound baby potatoes,
    quartered

1 clove garlic, halved
1 tablespoon extra–virgin
    olive oil
3 tablespoons melted butter
1 lemon, halved
1 bunch fresh thyme

---

1. Pat chicken dry and season all over with salt and pepper. Tie legs together and tuck wing tips under body of chicken. (If you have time, let rest in fridge for 1 hour, or up to overnight.)

2. Preheat oven to 425°. Fill a large baking baking dish with onion, carrots, celery, potatoes, and garlic. Toss with olive oil and season with salt and pepper. Place chicken on top.

3. Brush chicken all over with melted butter and stuff cavity with lemon and most of the thyme, reserving a couple sprigs for garnish.

4. Roast until juices run clear and a meat thermometer inserted into center of thigh reads 165°, 50 minutes to 1 hour. Tent chicken with foil and let rest 15 to 20 minutes, then transfer to a cutting board and carve.

5. Garnish with thyme leaves before serving with roasted vegetables.

CHICKEN BACON RANCH BUBBLE-UP BAKE

TOTAL TIME **1 HR**

SERVES 8

Bubble-up bake believers, we must confess that we took liberties here. Instead of mixing biscuit dough into the broccoli cheddar sauce, we used the biscuits as a topping. While not traditional, we promise the textural contrast is on point.

Cooking spray
6 slices bacon
6 tablespoons butter
6 tablespoons all-purpose flour

3 cups whole milk
3 cups shredded cheddar
2 large heads broccoli, cut into small florets
3 cups shredded chicken

1 (16.3-ounce) can refrigerated biscuits
2 teaspoons ranch seasoning mix

---

1. Preheat oven to 350°. Grease a 9x13-inch baking dish with cooking spray. In a large skillet, cook bacon until crispy, about 8 minutes, then drain on a paper towel-lined plate. Wipe skillet clean.

2. In the same skillet over medium heat, melt butter. Whisk in flour and cook until bubbly, about 1 minute. Gradually stir in milk and bring to a simmer. Cook until thickened, about 2 minutes. Whisk in cheese and cook until melted, 1 minute. Season with salt and pepper and stir in broccoli. Remove from heat.

3. Spread broccoli mixture into the bottom of the baking dish, then top with chicken. Cut each biscuit into eighths and scatter on top of chicken. Chop bacon into small pieces and scatter on top of biscuits, then sprinkle with ranch seasoning.

4. Bake until biscuits are golden and cooked through, about 25 minutes.

3

NEW DINNER
FAVORITES

NACHO CASSEROLE

TOTAL TIME
45 MIN

SERVES
6

If a pile of nachos and a burrito had a baby, this would be their casserole love child. Covered in a creamy cheddar cheese sauce, it's not for the faint of heart.

---

1 tablespoon extra-virgin olive oil

1 onion, chopped

1 pound ground beef

4 tablespoons all-purpose flour, divided

2 tablespoons tomato paste

1¾ cups chicken stock

1 (15-ounce) can tomato sauce

1 tablespoon chili powder

1 teaspoon ground cumin

¼ teaspoon paprika

Kosher salt

Freshly ground black pepper

3 cups cooked white rice

2½ cups shredded cheddar, divided

½ cup shredded Monterey jack

¼ cup sour cream

1 cup crushed tortilla chips

2 tablespoons butter

1 cup whole milk

¼ cup thinly sliced green onions, for garnish

Hot sauce, for serving

---

1. Preheat oven to 375°. In a large skillet over medium heat, heat oil. Sauté onion, stirring occasionally, until it begins to soften. Add beef, using a wooden spoon to break up meat, and cook until meat is no longer pink, 6 minutes. Drain fat.

2. Return skillet over medium heat, then stir 2 tablespoons flour into beef mixture. Cook 1 minute, then add tomato paste and stir to combine. Add chicken stock, tomato sauce, and spices and season with salt and pepper. Bring mixture to a simmer. Reduce heat to low and let simmer 10 minutes.

3. Transfer mixture to a medium casserole dish. Stir in cooked rice, ½ cup cheddar, Monterey jack, and sour cream. Top with tortilla chips and bake until chips are toasted and golden, about 15 minutes.

4. Meanwhile, make nacho cheese sauce: In a small saucepan over medium heat, melt butter. Whisk in remaining 2 tablespoons flour and cook for 1 minute. Whisk in milk and bring to a simmer. When milk begins to thicken, stir in remaining 2 cups cheddar, whisking constantly until sauce is smooth. Season with salt and pepper.

5. Pour cheese sauce over casserole then garnish with green onions and drizzle with hot sauce.

PHILLY CHEESESTEAK CASSEROLE

TOTAL TIME **40 MIN**

SERVES **6**

This is essentially a cheesesteak stuffing with hoagie croutons; not even your friends from Philly could refuse it.

Cooking spray

4 hoagie rolls, cut into
  1-inch cubes

4 tablespoons melted butter

1 teaspoon garlic powder

2 tablespoons extra-virgin
  olive oil, divided

1 onion, sliced

2 bell peppers, sliced

Kosher salt

Freshly ground black pepper

2 cloves garlic, minced

1½ pounds sirloin steak,
  sliced into strips

2 tablespoons Worcestershire
  sauce

12 slices provolone

1 cup low-sodium beef broth

Freshly chopped parsley,
  for garnish

---

1. Preheat oven to 350°. Grease a 9x13-inch baking dish with cooking spray. On a large baking sheet, toss hoagie roll cubes with melted butter and garlic powder. Bake until lightly golden, 15 minutes.

2. In a large skillet over medium heat, heat 1 tablespoon oil. Add onion and peppers and season with salt and pepper. Cook, stirring occasionally, until soft, 8 minutes. Stir in garlic and cook until fragrant, about 1 minute, then transfer mixture to a large bowl.

3. Increase heat to medium-high and heat remaining 1 tablespoon of oil. Add steak in a single layer, working in batches if necessary, then season with salt and pepper. Cook until steak is cooked through, 5 minutes for medium. Return vegetables to the skillet with steak and stir in Worcestershire. Remove from heat.

4. Spread half of hoagie roll cubes in prepared baking dish then add half the steak mixture. Top with 6 slices provolone. Add remaining cubes and steak, then pour broth over top. Top with remaining 6 slices provolone. Bake until cheese is melty, 12 minutes.

5. Garnish with parsley before serving.

CAPRESE QUINOA BAKE

TOTAL TIME
1 HR

SERVES 8

When this came out of the Delish test kitchen, everyone went capre–zy. Quinoa might not have been the first thing you thought of when you heard the word *casserole*, but it will be now.

1⅓ cups low–sodium chicken broth

1⅓ cups white quinoa

3 large tomatoes

2 cups baby spinach, tightly packed

1 tablespoon Italian seasoning

½ cup freshly grated Parmesan

2 garlic cloves, minced

Kosher salt

Freshly ground black pepper

1 (16–ounce) ball fresh mozzarella, sliced

¼ cup freshly sliced basil, for garnish

---

1. Preheat oven to 400°. Using chicken broth, prepare quinoa according to package instructions.

2. Chop 1 tomato into medium pieces. In a 9x13–inch baking dish, combine cooked quinoa, chopped tomato, spinach, Italian seasoning, Parmesan, and garlic and season with salt and pepper. Spread into an even layer.

3. Top quinoa mixture with sliced tomatoes and mozzarella.

4. Bake until cheese is melty and slightly golden, 30 minutes.

5. Garnish with basil before serving.

PRO TIP!

Look for low-moisture fresh mozzarella in your grocery store. It'll release less water.

BAKED SHRIMP SCAMPI

TOTAL TIME 25 MIN

SERVES 6

PSA: If you're not dipping a crusty baguette into the garlicky juices left over at the bottom of the pan, you're doing it wrong.

---

3 pounds shrimp, peeled and deveined
4 tablespoons melted butter
¼ cup dry white wine
Juice and zest of 2 lemons, plus wedges for serving

2 shallots, minced
4 cloves garlic, minced
6 tablespoons freshly chopped parsley, divided
¼ teaspoon crushed red pepper flakes

Kosher salt
Freshly ground black pepper
⅓ cup panko bread crumbs
¼ cup extra-virgin olive oil
Crusty bread, for serving

---

1. Preheat oven to 425°. In a large bowl, combine shrimp, melted butter, white wine, lemon juice and zest, shallots, garlic, 2 tablespoons parsley, and red pepper flakes and season with salt and pepper.

2. Place shrimp in a 9x13–inch baking dish. In a medium bowl, mix bread crumbs with oil and remaining 4 tablespoons parsley and season with salt and pepper. Sprinkle panko mixture over shrimp.

3. Bake until shrimp are opaque, 12 to 15 minutes. Serve with lemon wedges and bread.

HONEY DIJON ROASTED SALMON

TOTAL TIME
30 MIN

SERVES 6

Roasting a whole salmon fillet gives you perfectly flaky salmon with low risk of overcooking, every 👏 single 👏 time 👏 .

Cooking spray
1 lemon, sliced
1 (3-pound) salmon fillet
Kosher salt
Freshly ground black pepper
½ cup whole-grain mustard
¼ cup extra-virgin olive oil
¼ cup honey
2 cloves garlic, minced
½ teaspoon crushed red
   pepper flakes
Freshly chopped parsley,
   for garnish

1. Preheat oven to 400° and grease a large baking dish with cooking spray.

2. Place lemon slices on bottom of dish and salmon on top. Season with salt and pepper.

3. In a medium bowl, whisk together mustard, oil, honey, garlic, and red pepper flakes and season with salt and pepper. Pour sauce over salmon.

4. Roast until salmon is cooked through and flakes easily with a fork, 20 minutes.

5. Heat broiler and broil until caramelized, 5 minutes more.

6. Garnish with parsley before serving.

CAULIFLOWER BAKED "ZITI"

TOTAL TIME 1 HR 10 MIN

SERVES 6

Ok, *fine*. There's not actually any ziti in this recipe, but you honestly won't even care. The roasted cauliflower does an excellent job of replacing the pasta.

---

2 medium heads cauliflower, cut into florets
3 tablespoons extra-virgin olive oil, divided
Kosher salt
Freshly ground black pepper
1 medium onion, chopped

2 cloves garlic, minced
Pinch red pepper flakes
1 pound ground beef
2 tablespoons tomato paste
1 teaspoon dried oregano
1 (28-ounce) can crushed tomatoes

2 tablespoons freshly sliced basil, plus more for garnish
1½ cups ricotta
2 cups shredded mozzarella, divided
½ cup freshly grated Parmesan

---

1. Preheat oven to 425°. Roast cauliflower: Spread cauliflower florets on two large baking sheets. Drizzle with 2 tablespoons olive oil and season with salt and pepper. Bake until cauliflower is tender and turning golden around edges, about 20 minutes. Decrease oven temperature to 375°.

2. Make sauce: In a large pot over medium heat, heat remaining 1 tablespoon oil. Add onion and cook until soft, about 5 minutes. Stir in garlic and red pepper flakes and cook until fragrant, 1 minute more. Add ground beef and cook, breaking up meat with a wooden spoon, until no longer pink, about 6 minutes. Drain fat.

3. Add tomato paste and oregano to beef mixture. Cook until slightly darkened, 2 minutes. Add crushed tomatoes and bring sauce to a simmer; then reduce heat and cook, stirring occasionally, until flavors have melded, 10 to 15 minutes. Season with salt and pepper and stir in basil.

4. In a large bowl, combine sauce with cauliflower. Place half the cauliflower in an even layer in a 9x13-inch baking dish. Dollop ricotta on top and sprinkle with 1 cup mozzarella and Parmesan. Add remaining cauliflower and top with remaining 1 cup mozzarella.

5. Bake until cheese is melty and golden, about 28 minutes.

6. Garnish with basil before serving.

PERFECT BAKED MEATBALLS

TOTAL TIME
55 MIN

SERVES
4

Hot take: Baked meatballs are better than fried. We'll admit that they're not as crusty. But simmered in the sauce (in the oven) and covered with cheese, they're tender as hell and incredibly delicious.

FOR THE SAUCE
¼ cup extra-virgin olive oil
2 cloves garlic, minced
2 tablespoons freshly chopped oregano
1 (28-ounce) can crushed tomatoes
Kosher salt
Freshly ground black pepper

FOR THE MEATBALLS
1½ pounds ground beef
½ cup bread crumbs
½ cup freshly grated Parmesan, divided
2 tablespoons freshly chopped parsley, plus more for garnish
2 cloves garlic, minced
1 large egg
½ teaspoon crushed red pepper flakes
Kosher salt
Freshly ground black pepper
⅓ cup shredded mozzarella
Freshly sliced basil, for garnish

1. Preheat oven to 375°. Make sauce: In a large pot over low heat, heat oil. Add garlic and oregano and cook, stirring constantly, until fragrant, about 1 minute. Add tomatoes and season with salt and pepper. Let simmer while you form meatballs.

2. Make meatballs: In a large bowl, combine beef, bread crumbs, ¼ cup Parmesan, parsley, garlic, egg, and red pepper flakes and season with salt and pepper. Thoroughly combine, then form into 2-inch meatballs. Transfer to a 9x13-inch baking dish.

3. Bake 20 minutes, then toss with sauce and sprinkle with mozzarella and remaining ¼ cup Parmesan. Return to oven and bake until cheese is melty and meatballs are cooked through, 15 minutes more.

4. Garnish with basil before serving.

PRO TIP!

If you're short on time, skip homemade sauce and use a 32-ounce jar of marinara instead.

BEEF ENCHILADAS

TOTAL TIME
40 MIN

MAKES
8

Turns out delicious enchiladas are insanely easy to make at home. The secret: canned enchilada sauce. When it's so good, there's no point in making it from scratch—especially on a weeknight.

1 tablespoon extra-virgin olive oil

½ medium onion, chopped

2 cloves garlic, minced

1 pound ground beef

1 teaspoon chili powder

1 teaspoon cumin

Kosher salt

Freshly ground black pepper

1 (19-ounce) can enchilada sauce

1 (15-ounce) can corn, drained

1 (15-ounce) can black beans, drained and rinsed

8 medium flour tortillas

⅔ cup shredded Monterey jack

⅓ cup shredded cheddar

TOPPINGS

Quartered grape tomatoes

Diced avocado

Finely chopped onion

Fresh cilantro leaves

1. Preheat oven to 350°. In a large skillet over medium heat, heat oil. Add onion and cook until soft, 5 minutes. Stir in garlic and cook until fragrant, 1 minute more. Add ground beef and cook until no longer pink, about 6 minutes. Drain fat.

2. Stir chili powder and cumin into beef mixture and season with salt and pepper. Stir in enchilada sauce, then remove from heat and stir in corn and black beans.

3. Spoon meat mixture into center of each tortilla and roll up. Place rolled-up tortillas side by side in a 9x13-inch baking dish and top with cheeses.

4. Bake until cheese is melty, 15 to 18 minutes.

5. Garnish with tomatoes, avocado, onion, and cilantro.

SAUSAGE & PEPPERS BAKE

TOTAL TIME
55 MIN

SERVES 6

Nothing could be more low fuss than this throw-everything-in-the-pan dinner. The garlicky oil mixture adds a ton of bold flavor to the peppers and onions, so don't skip it!

3 tablespoons extra-virgin olive oil
1 tablespoon red wine vinegar
2 cloves garlic, minced
2 teaspoons dried oregano
1 teaspoon crushed red pepper
3 bell peppers, sliced
1 large yellow onion, sliced
Kosher salt
Freshly ground black pepper
6 sweet or hot Italian sausages, sliced into quarters
¼ cup freshly sliced basil

1. Preheat oven to 400°. In a large bowl, whisk together oil, vinegar, garlic, oregano, and red pepper. Add peppers and onions to the bowl and toss to coat in oil mixture. Season with salt and pepper, then transfer to a large baking dish. Scatter sausage pieces on top of vegetables.

2. Bake until vegetables are tender and sausage is cooked through, 40 to 45 minutes.

3. Top with basil and serve hot.

PRO TIP!
If you'd like a crispy topping, mix together:

½ cup panko bread crumbs
2 tablespoons extra-virgin
    olive oil
2 tablespoons freshly grated
    Parmesan
1 tablespoon chopped parsley

Sprinkle it over the casserole before baking.

MEATBALL SUB CASSEROLE

TOTAL TIME 45 MIN

SERVES 6

One taste tester said this casserole reminded him of a meatball sub that's been wrapped in foil. The bread has steamed and softened a bit and the sauce has soaked through. Trust us, this is a *very* good thing.

FOR THE MEATBALLS
1 pound ground beef
2 cloves garlic, minced
1 large egg
⅓ cup bread crumbs
2 tablespoons freshly
  chopped parsley, plus
  more for garnish
Kosher salt

Freshly ground black pepper
1 tablespoon vegetable oil

FOR THE CASSEROLE
Cooking spray
1 baguette, sliced ¾-inch
  thick
4 tablespoons (½ stick)
  melted butter

2 cloves garlic, minced
1 teaspoon Italian seasoning
Kosher salt
Freshly ground black pepper
2 cups freshly shredded
  mozzarella, divided
3 cups marinara sauce

---

1. Preheat oven to 400°. Make meatballs: In a large bowl, combine ground beef, garlic, egg, bread crumbs, and parsley. Season generously with salt and pepper, then stir together until just combined. Form into 30 evenly sized balls.

2. In a large skillet over medium-high heat, heat oil. Cook meatballs in batches, 6 minutes, then drain on a paper towel-lined plate.

3. Grease a 9x13-inch baking dish with cooking spray. Place baguette slices in an even layer in bottom of dish. In a medium bowl, stir together melted butter, garlic, and Italian seasoning and season with salt and pepper. Brush all over baguette slices. Top with 1 cup mozzarella, an even layer of marinara, meatballs, and remaining mozzarella.

4. Bake until cheese is melty, 12 to 15 minutes. Garnish with parsley before serving.

CORNBREAD CASSEROLE

TOTAL TIME
1 HR 15 MIN

SERVES
8

We ❤️ Jiffy cornbread mix, particularly when it sits atop a perfect beef chili. Test kitchen tip: Ignore the instructions on the back of the box and stir frozen corn, sour cream, and melted butter into the mix along with the eggs.

FOR THE CHILI
1 tablespoon extra-virgin olive oil
½ onion, chopped
3 cloves garlic, minced
2 tablespoons tomato paste
1 pound ground beef
1 tablespoon chili powder
1 teaspoon ground cumin
1 teaspoon dried oregano

Kosher salt
Freshly ground black pepper
1 (15-ounce) can kidney beans, drained
1 (28-ounce) crushed tomatoes

FOR THE CORNBREAD
2 boxes Jiffy corn muffin mix
1 cup frozen corn

1 cup sour cream
4 tablespoons butter, melted
2 large eggs

FOR THE TOPPING
Sour cream
Shredded cheddar
Sliced green onions

1. Preheat oven to 400°. In a large pot over medium heat, heat oil. Add onion and cook until soft, 5 minutes. Stir in garlic and cook until fragrant, 1 minute more, then add tomato paste, stirring to combine. Add ground beef and cook until no longer pink. Drain fat.

2. Return beef mixture to skillet and add chili powder, cumin, and oregano and season with salt and pepper. Add kidney beans and crushed tomatoes. Bring chili to a boil, then reduce heat and let simmer, 20 minutes.

3. Meanwhile, make cornbread: In a medium bowl, whisk together corn muffin mix, corn, sour cream, melted butter, and eggs until evenly combined.

4. Pour chili into a 9x13-inch baking dish. Top with cornbread batter and spread in an even layer. Bake until a toothpick inserted into center of cornbread comes out clean, 20 to 25 minutes. Serve topped with sour cream, cheddar, and green onions.

CHILI CHEESE DOG CASSEROLE

TOTAL TIME

40 MIN

SERVES
8

We took a lot of shortcuts with this recipe—Refrigerated crescent dough! Canned chili!—but if you have some extra time (or chili) on your hands, you can fancy it up with the homemade stuff instead.

1 (8–ounce) tube refrigerated crescent dough

1 cup shredded cheddar

8 hot dogs

2 (15–ounce) cans chili

2 tablespoons melted butter

1 teaspoon finely chopped chives, plus more for garnish

½ teaspoon garlic powder

1. Preheat oven to 375°. Unroll crescent dough and pinch together seams to seal. Slice into 8 even squares. Sprinkle each square with cheese and top with a hot dog. Roll up each and pinch edges to seal.

2. Spread chili in an even layer on bottom of a 9x13–inch baking dish. Place hot dogs in a row side by side on top.

3. In a small bowl, stir together melted butter, chives, and garlic powder. Brush all over hot dogs.

4. Bake until dough is golden and cooked through, 30 minutes. (Cover with foil if it begins to get too dark.)

5. Garnish with chives before serving.

CHAPTER

4

NOODLES
& PASTAS

LOBSTER MAC & CHEESE

TOTAL TIME
40 MIN

SERVES
8

Oh, you fancy, huh? Curly cavatappi + fontina + lobster + crispy panko bread crumbs majorly upgrade your everyday macaroni and cheese. Make this for someone you really want to impress.

---

1 pound cavatappi
4 tablespoons butter
¼ cup all-purpose flour
2½ cups whole milk
Pinch nutmeg (optional)
Kosher salt
Freshly ground black pepper

1½ cups shredded white cheddar
1 cup shredded Fontina
¾ cup freshly grated Parmesan, divided
1 pound cooked lobster, roughly chopped

½ cup panko bread crumbs
1 tablespoon extra-virgin olive oil
Freshly chopped parsley, for garnish

---

1. Preheat oven to 375°. In a large pot of salted boiling water, cook cavatappi according to package directions until al dente. Drain.

2. In a large saucepan over medium heat, melt butter. Sprinkle with flour and cook until slightly golden, 2 to 3 minutes. Pour in milk and whisk until combined. Season with nutmeg (if using), salt, and pepper. Let simmer until thickened slightly, about 2 minutes.

3. Remove pan from heat and stir in cheddar, Fontina, and ½ cup Parmesan and whisk until melty and smooth. Fold in cooked cavatappi and lobster, then transfer to a 9x13-inch baking dish.

4. In a medium bowl, stir together panko, remaining ¼ cup Parmesan, and oil and season with salt and pepper. Sprinkle over pasta.

5. Bake until bubbly and golden, 20 to 25 minutes.

6. Let stand 10 minutes, then garnish with parsley before serving.

CAPRESE CHICKEN LASAGNA

TOTAL TIME
50 MIN

SERVES
6

If you couldn't already tell, we're big fans of caprese and of reimagining classics with big and unexpected flavors.

1 pound lasagna noodles, cooked

1 tablespoon extra-virgin olive oil

1 pound boneless skinless chicken breasts, cut into pieces

2 teaspoons dried oregano

Kosher salt

Freshly ground black pepper

2 tablespoons balsamic vinegar

3 cloves garlic, minced, divided

3 tablespoons butter

3 tablespoons all-purpose flour

2½ cups whole milk

¾ cup freshly grated Parmesan

5 cups shredded mozzarella, divided

1 (16-ounce) container ricotta

1 large egg

4 roma tomatoes, thinly sliced

½ cup thinly sliced basil leaves, plus more for garnish

Balsamic glaze, for drizzling

1. In a large skillet over medium heat, heat oil. Season chicken with oregano, salt, and pepper. Cook until golden, 8 minutes. Add balsamic vinegar and half of garlic to pan and stir until combined. Transfer to a plate.

2. Make sauce: Bring skillet back to medium heat and melt butter. Add remaining garlic and cook until fragrant, 1 minute. Add flour and cook until golden, 1 minute more. Add milk and simmer until thick and creamy, 3 minutes, then add Parmesan and 1 cup mozzarella. Season with salt and pepper.

3. In a small bowl, stir together ricotta and egg and season with salt and pepper.

4. In a 9x13-inch baking dish, spread a thin layer of sauce. Add a layer of lasagna noodles, slightly overlapping, and top with about a third of ricotta mixture, a third of tomatoes, a third of basil, a third of cooked chicken, another layer of sauce, and a third of mozzarella. Repeat for a total of three layers, ending with mozzarella.

5. Bake until bubbly and golden, 25 to 30 minutes. Garnish with basil and drizzle with balsamic glaze before serving.

ITALIAN MAC & CHEESE

TOTAL TIME
1 HR

SERVES
4

The first time we made this one-pot mac & cheese, we couldn't help but eat it straight from the pot. But after much debate and consideration, we decided that adding cheese and baking it could only improve the situation. And we were right.

1 pound Italian sausage (hot or sweet), casings removed
1 large onion, diced
2 cloves garlic, minced
1 red bell pepper, diced
12 ounces cavatappi

1 (16-ounce) jar marinara
4 cups low-sodium chicken broth
Kosher salt
¼ cup half-and-half or heavy cream

2 cups shredded mozzarella, divided
Freshly chopped parsley, for garnish

1. Preheat oven to 350°. In a large skillet over medium-high heat, cook sausage, breaking up with a wooden spoon, until seared and no longer pink, about 4 minutes. Add onion, garlic, and bell pepper and cook, stirring, until soft, 5 minutes more.

2. Add cavatappi and stir until coated, then pour marinara and broth over top and season with salt. Bring liquid to a boil, then reduce heat to medium-low and simmer until pasta is al dente and almost all liquid has been absorbed, about 25 minutes.

3. Stir in half-and-half and simmer until mostly absorbed, 2 minutes more. Remove from heat and stir in 1 cup mozzarella.

4. Transfer mixture to a large baking dish and sprinkle with remaining 1 cup mozzarella. Bake until cheese is bubbly and golden, about 10 minutes.

5. Garnish with parsley before serving.

RAVIOLI LASAGNA

TOTAL TIME
1 HR **10** MIN

SERVES
6

Your favorite stuffed pasta became one with your favorite pasta casserole proving that dreams really do come true.

Cooking spray

1 tablespoon extra–virgin olive oil

½ medium onion, chopped

1 pound ground beef

Kosher salt

Freshly ground black pepper

2 cloves garlic, minced

1 (32–ounce) jar marinara

1 (16–ounce) container ricotta

1 large egg

1 cup freshly grated Parmesan, divided

¼ cup freshly chopped basil, plus more for garnish

1 teaspoon garlic powder

2 (12–ounce) packages frozen cheese ravioli

3 cups shredded mozzarella

1. Preheat oven to 350° and grease a 9x13–inch baking dish with cooking spray. In a large skillet over medium heat, heat oil. Add onion and cook until soft, 5 minutes. Add ground beef and cook, breaking up meat with a wooden spoon, until no longer pink, about 8 minutes. Drain fat.

2. Return beef mixture to skillet and season with salt and pepper. Stir in garlic and marinara, then reduce heat and simmer for 5 minutes.

3. Meanwhile, in a medium bowl, combine ricotta, egg, ¼ cup Parmesan, basil, and garlic powder and season with salt and pepper.

4. Spread one–third of meat sauce in prepared baking dish. Top with a single layer of ravioli, half the remaining meat sauce, half the ricotta mixture, half the mozzarella, half the remaining Parmesan. Repeat layers, ending on cheeses.

5. Cover pan loosely with aluminum foil and bake 30 minutes. Remove foil and bake until golden and bubbly, 15 more minutes.

6. Garnish with basil before serving.

TURKEY TETRAZZINI

TOTAL TIME
1 HR 25 MIN

SERVES 8

The definition of a cozy winter dinner, this classic casserole is the perfect dish to make with leftover turkey, especially when you're hosting out-of-town guests for the holidays.

Cooking spray
1 pound spaghetti
6 tablespoons butter, divided
2 cloves garlic, minced
1 pound sliced baby bella mushrooms
½ cup white wine
¼ cup all-purpose flour

2½ cups low-sodium chicken broth
1 cup heavy cream
Kosher salt
Freshly ground black pepper
2 pounds leftover roast turkey, chopped (about 5 cups)

1 cup shredded white cheddar
1 cup frozen peas
1 teaspoon dried oregano
1 cup panko bread crumbs
½ cup freshly grated Parmesan
2 tablespoons extra-virgin olive oil

---

1. Preheat oven to 350° and grease a 9x13-inch baking dish with cooking spray.

2. In a large pot of boiling salted water, cook spaghetti according to package directions. Drain.

3. In a large skillet over medium heat, melt 2 tablespoons butter. Add garlic and cook until fragrant, 1 minute. Add mushrooms and wine and cook until most of wine is absorbed and mushrooms are soft, 5 minutes.

4. Add remaining 4 tablespoons butter to skillet, then whisk in flour and cook until golden, 3 minutes. Slowly add broth and cream and whisk until no lumps remain. Simmer until thickened, 5 minutes. Season with salt and pepper.

5. Add turkey, cheese, peas, and oregano and toss until combined. Add cooked spaghetti and toss to coat. Season with salt and pepper then transfer mixture to prepared dish.

6. In a medium bowl, toss to combine panko, Parmesan, and oil. Top baking dish evenly with panko mixture. Bake until top is golden and cheese is melty, 25 minutes. Let cool 10 minutes before serving.

PRO TIP!

Leftover rotisserie chicken works well in this recipe too!

CHICKEN POT PIE NOODLES

TOTAL TIME
1 HR 10 MIN

SERVES
8

Not everyone can pull off a chicken pot pie (the crust can be tricky!). But we're very serious when we say anyone can master these creamy, vegetable–studded noodles.

12 ounces egg noodles
2 tablespoons butter
2 carrots, peeled and diced
2 stalks celery, diced
1 large onion, chopped
2 cloves garlic, minced
Kosher salt
Freshly ground black pepper

2 tablespoons all–purpose flour
2 cups low–sodium chicken broth
2 cups heavy cream
2 cups cooked shredded chicken
½ cup frozen corn
½ cup frozen peas

½ cup panko bread crumbs
2 tablespoons freshly grated Parmesan
1 tablespoon extra–virgin olive oil
Freshly chopped parsley, for garnish

1. Preheat oven to 375°. In a large pot of salted boiling water, cook noodles 5 minutes. Drain.

2. Meanwhile, in a large skillet over medium heat, melt butter. Add carrots, celery, onion, and garlic and season with salt and pepper. Cook until softened, 3 minutes, then stir in flour and cook 1 minute.

3. Stir in broth and heavy cream and bring to a boil. Reduce heat and simmer, stirring occasionally, until thickened, 3 minutes.

4. Remove from heat and stir in cooked noodles, chicken, corn, and peas. Transfer mixture to a 9x13–inch baking dish.

5. In a small bowl, stir together panko, Parmesan, and oil and season with salt and pepper. Sprinkle on top of noodle mixture and bake until golden, 25 to 28 minutes.

6. Garnish with parsley before serving.

CLASSIC BAKED ZITI

TOTAL TIME
1 HR
5 MIN

SERVES
6

The key to any great baked pasta: the sauce. Ours is nothing fancy, but it's exactly what you want when you're in the mood for this classic.

---

1 pound ziti
1 tablespoon extra-virgin olive oil
1 medium onion, chopped
2 cloves garlic, minced
Pinch crushed red pepper flakes

1 pound ground beef
Kosher salt
Freshly ground black pepper
2 tablespoons tomato paste
1 teaspoon dried oregano
1 (28-ounce) can crushed tomatoes

2 tablespoons thinly sliced basil, plus whole leaves for garnish
1½ cups ricotta
2 cups shredded mozzarella
½ cup freshly grated Parmesan

---

1. Preheat oven to 350°. In a large pot of boiling salted water, cook ziti according to package directions until al dente. Drain.

2. In a large saucepan over medium heat, heat oil. Add onion and cook until soft, 5 minutes. Stir in garlic and red pepper flakes and cook until fragrant, 1 minute more. Add ground beef and season with salt and pepper. Cook, breaking up meat with a wooden spoon, until no longer pink, about 6 minutes. Drain fat.

3. Return beef mixture to saucepan, then stir in tomato paste and oregano and cook 2 minutes. Add crushed tomatoes and season with salt and pepper. Bring sauce to a simmer, then reduce heat and cook, stirring occasionally, until slightly reduced and flavors have melded, 10 minutes. Remove from heat and stir in basil.

4. In a large bowl, toss cooked ziti with sauce until coated. Fold in ricotta, leaving large clumps. Transfer half the pasta mixture to a 9x13-inch baking dish and sprinkle with half of both the mozzarella and Parmesan. Top with remaining pasta mixture and cheeses.

5. Cover baking dish with foil and bake until cheese is melty and bubbly, 20 to 25 minutes.

6. Garnish with basil leaves before serving.

CHICKEN ALFREDO BAKE

TOTAL TIME
55 MIN

SERVES
6

Having "just a little bit" is literally impossible. Don't say we didn't warn you.

---

1 pound penne
4 tablespoons butter, plus more for baking dish
2 tablespoons extra-virgin olive oil
1 pound boneless skinless chicken breasts

1 teaspoon Italian seasoning
Kosher salt
Freshly ground black pepper
2 cloves garlic, minced
4 tablespoons all-purpose flour
3 cups half-and-half

½ cup freshly grated Parmesan
1 cup shredded mozzarella
Freshly chopped parsley, for garnish

---

1. In a large pot of salted boiling water, cook penne according to package directions until al dente. Drain. Preheat oven to 350° and butter a 9x13-inch baking dish.

2. In a large skillet over medium heat, heat oil. Season chicken with Italian seasoning, salt, and pepper. Add to skillet and cook until golden and no longer pink, 8 minutes per side. Transfer to a cutting board and let rest 5 minutes before slicing into strips. Wipe skillet clean.

3. Make sauce: Return skillet to medium heat and melt butter. Add garlic and cook until fragrant, about 1 minute, then whisk in flour and cook until golden, 1 minute more. Gradually pour in half-and-half, whisking constantly.

4. Bring mixture to a simmer and stir in Parmesan. Simmer until thick, about 1 minute, then season with salt and pepper.

5. In a large bowl, combine cooked penne, chicken, and alfredo sauce. Spread about half of pasta mixture in prepared baking dish, then sprinkle with half of mozzarella. Add remaining pasta mixture and mozzarella.

6. Bake until cheese is melty, 12 to 15 minutes.

7. Garnish with parsley before serving.

TUSCAN BUTTER GNOCCHI

TOTAL TIME
45 MIN

SERVES 8

Tuscan butter is a garlicky cream sauce made with heavy cream, bursting cherry tomatoes, grated Parmesan, and wilted spinach. It's a Delish classic, and soon to be your favorite sauce.

---

4 tablespoons butter
3 cloves garlic, minced
2 cups halved cherry tomatoes
1 teaspoon dried oregano
Kosher salt
Freshly ground black pepper

Pinch red pepper flakes
4 cups baby spinach
1 cup low-sodium chicken broth
1 cup heavy cream
½ cup freshly grated Parmesan

¼ cup freshly chopped herbs (such as basil and parsley), plus more for garnish
2 (17.5-ounce) packages gnocchi
1 cup shredded mozzarella
Lemon wedges, for serving

---

1. Preheat oven to 350°. In a large skillet over medium heat, melt butter. Add garlic and cook until fragrant, 1 minute. Add cherry tomatoes and season with oregano, salt, pepper, and red pepper flakes. Cook until tomatoes are beginning to burst then add spinach and cook until beginning to wilt.

2. Stir in broth, heavy cream, Parmesan, and herbs and bring to a simmer. Reduce heat to low and simmer until sauce is slightly reduced, about 3 minutes.

3. Add gnocchi and toss to coat. Pour gnocchi into a 9x13-inch baking pan and top with mozzarella. Bake until gnocchi is cooked through and cheese is melty, 30 minutes.

4. Garnish with more herbs and squeeze lemon on top before serving.

CLASSIC LASAGNA

TOTAL TIME
1 HR 10 MIN

SERVES 8

Everyone should know how to make a good lasagna, and this one is exceptional. Use your favorite marinara sauce here (jarred or homemade); it'll make all the difference.

¾ pound lasagna noodles

1 teaspoon extra–virgin olive oil, plus more for drizzling

2 pounds ground beef

4 cloves garlic, minced

2 teaspoons dried oregano

Kosher salt

Freshly ground black pepper

2 (32–ounce) jars marinara

1 (16–ounce) container whole milk ricotta

½ cup freshly grated Parmesan, divided

¼ cup chopped parsley, plus more for garnish

2 pounds sliced mozzarella

---

1. Preheat oven to 375°. In a large pot of salted boiling water, cook pasta according to package directions until al dente. Drain and drizzle a bit of olive oil to prevent noodles from sticking together.

2. Meanwhile, in a large pot over medium–high heat, heat oil. Cook ground beef until no longer pink, breaking up with a wooden spoon, then drain fat. Return beef to skillet and add garlic and oregano and stir for 1 minute. Season with salt and pepper, then add marinara and stir until warmed through.

3. Combine ricotta, ¼ cup Parmesan, and parsley in a large mixing bowl and season with salt and pepper. Set aside.

4. In a 9x13–inch dish, evenly spread a quarter of the meat sauce across the bottom of the dish, then top with a single layer of lasagna noodles, a layer of ricotta mixture, and a single layer of mozzarella. Repeat layers, topping the last layer of noodles with meat sauce, Parmesan, and mozzarella.

5. Cover with foil and bake for 15 minutes, then increase temperature to 400° and bake uncovered for 18 to 20 minutes.

6. Garnish with parsley before serving.

CHAPTER

5

HEALTHY

COMFORT
FOOD

BUFFALO ROASTED CAULIFLOWER

TOTAL TIME
1 HR
40 MIN

SERVES
4

Think of whole roasted cauliflower as the vegetarian version of roast chicken. (It's so good, we even make it for Thanksgiving dinner.) This buffalo take is just as good for a healthy weeknight dinner as it is for Sunday night football. Just make sure you have plenty of ranch dressing to go around!

- 3 stalks celery, 2 roughly chopped and 1 diced
- 2 large carrots, roughly chopped
- 1 medium onion, cut into wedges
- 1 tablespoon extra–virgin olive oil
- Kosher salt
- Freshly ground black pepper
- 1 large head cauliflower
- 5 tablespoons melted butter
- ⅓ cup hot sauce (such as Frank's)
- ½ teaspoon garlic powder
- ¼ cup ranch dressing, for serving
- ¼ cup crumbled blue cheese, for serving
- 1 tablespoon freshly chopped chives, for serving

---

1. Preheat oven to 400°. In a large baking dish, toss chopped celery, carrots, and onion with oil and season with salt and pepper. Cut leaves and stem from cauliflower so it sits flat and place over vegetables.

2. Make buffalo sauce: In a small bowl, whisk together melted butter, hot sauce, and garlic powder and season with salt and pepper. Reserve ¼ cup for serving, then drizzle remaining buffalo sauce over cauliflower and brush evenly to coat.

3. Roast until cauliflower is golden and tender, about 1 hour 25 minutes.

4. Drizzle roasted cauliflower with ranch dressing and reserved buffalo sauce and sprinkle with blue cheese, diced celery, and chives.

LOADED CAULI "MAC"

TOTAL TIME 1 HR

MAKES 8

Basically, mac & cheese minus the mac. Plus so much bacon. Because there was never a dish that bacon didn't make 1,000 times better.

---

2 small heads cauliflower, cut into florets
2 tablespoons butter
3 cloves garlic, minced
3 tablespoons all-purpose flour

2 cups whole milk
2 ounces cream cheese
1½ cups shredded cheddar, divided
Kosher salt
Freshly ground black pepper

6 slices bacon, cooked and crumbled
¼ cup sliced green onions

---

1. Preheat oven to 350°. In a large pot of salted boiling water, blanch cauliflower, 3 minutes. Drain well.

2. Make cheese sauce: In a large skillet, melt butter. Add garlic and cook until fragrant, 1 minute, then add flour and stir until golden, 2 minutes. Add milk and bring to a low simmer, then add cream cheese, whisking until combined. Remove from heat and stir in 1 cup cheddar until melty. Season with salt and pepper.

3. In a large bowl, stir together drained cauliflower, cheese sauce, and all but 1 tablespoon each cooked bacon and green onions until combined.

4. Transfer mixture to a 9x13-inch baking dish and top with remaining ½ cup cheddar, bacon, and green onions.

5. Bake until cauliflower is tender and cheese is melty, 30 minutes.

6. Let cool slightly before serving.

ZUCCHINI BURRITO BOATS

TOTAL TIME
45 MIN

MAKES
6

When the craving for a burrito strikes, there's no denying it. Stuffing all your favorite fillings into a zucchini boat isn't exactly the same, but it's a damn good compromise.

---

3 zucchini, halved lengthwise
2 tablespoons extra-virgin olive oil, divided
Kosher salt
Freshly ground black pepper
½ onion, chopped
2 cloves garlic, minced

1 pound ground beef
½ teaspoon chili powder
½ teaspoon ground cumin
¼ teaspoon paprika
½ cup black beans
½ cup chopped cherry tomatoes

½ cup corn
1 cup shredded cheddar
1 cup shredded Monterey jack
Freshly chopped cilantro, for garnish

---

1. Preheat oven to 350°. Score zucchini (like you're dicing an avocado) and scoop out insides; set aside. Place zucchini halves cut-side up in a 9x13-inch baking dish and drizzle with 1 tablespoon oil. Season with salt and pepper.

2. Bake until zucchini turns bright green and just begins to soften, 10 minutes.

3. In a large skillet over medium heat, heat remaining 1 tablespoon of oil. Add onion and reserved zucchini and cook until soft, about 5 minutes. Stir in garlic and cook until fragrant, about 1 minute more. Add ground beef and cook, breaking up meat with a wooden spoon, until no longer pink, about 6 minutes. Drain fat.

4. Return beef mixture to skillet and stir in chili powder, cumin, and paprika, then season with salt and pepper. Stir in black beans, cherry tomatoes, and corn.

5. Spoon beef mixture into zucchini and top with cheeses.

6. Bake until zucchini is just tender and cheeses are melty, about 15 minutes.

7. Garnish with cilantro before serving.

SWEET POTATO LASAGNA

TOTAL TIME
1 HR 45 MIN

SERVES
12

In the world of lasagnas, there are no rules. If you want to replace the noodles with zucchini (page 105) or eggplant (page 110) or sweet potato, we're here for you. Always and forever.

Cooking spray
2 tablespoons extra-virgin olive oil
1 large onion, chopped
2 cloves garlic, minced
1 pound sweet Italian sausage, casings removed
Kosher salt

Freshly ground black pepper
2 cups marinara
1 (5-ounce) package baby spinach
1 (16-ounce) container ricotta
1 large egg, beaten
¾ cup grated Parmesan, divided

1 teaspoon dried oregano
3 large sweet potatoes, peeled and sliced ⅛-inch thick (about 2 pounds)
1½ cups shredded mozzarella
Freshly chopped parsley, for serving

1. Preheat oven to 375° and grease a 9x13-inch baking dish with cooking spray. In a large skillet over medium heat, heat oil. Add onion and cook until soft, 5 minutes, then add garlic and cook, 1 minute more. Add sausage and cook, 6 minutes. Season with salt and pepper. Pour in marinara sauce and bring to a simmer, then add spinach and cook until spinach is wilted. Remove from heat.

2. In a large bowl, stir together ricotta, egg, ½ cup Parmesan, and oregano. Season with salt and pepper.

3. Layer sweet potatoes in bottom of prepared baking dish, slightly overlapping. Spread about one-third of ricotta mixture over sweet potatoes then pour one-third of meat sauce on top. Repeat to make two more layers. Top lasagna with mozzarella and remaining ¼ cup Parmesan.

4. Cover with aluminum foil and bake until sweet potatoes are almost cooked through, about 45 minutes, then remove foil and bake until sweet potatoes are fork tender, 15 minutes more. Let rest 10 minutes.

5. Garnish with parsley before serving.

CABBAGE ENCHILADAS

TOTAL TIME
50
MIN

SERVES
4

It's official. Cabbage is cool again. Once we used a blanched large leaf to make a low-carb wrap, there was no turning back. The enchilada game was changed forever.

---

10 green cabbage leaves
1 tablespoon extra-virgin olive oil
1 large onion, chopped
1 red bell pepper, chopped
Kosher salt
2 cloves garlic, minced

2 teaspoons ground cumin
2 teaspoons chili powder
4 cups cooked shredded chicken
1⅓ cups red enchilada sauce, divided

2 tablespoons freshly chopped cilantro, plus more for garnish
1 cup shredded Monterey jack
½ cup shredded cheddar
½ cup sour cream
Juice of 1 lime

---

1. Preheat oven to 350°. Bring a large pot of water to a boil. Using tongs, dip each cabbage leaf in water for 30 seconds, then transfer to a paper towel-lined plate to dry.

2. In a large skillet over medium heat, heat oil. Add onion and bell pepper and season with salt. Cook until soft, 5 minutes, then stir in garlic, cumin, and chili powder and cook 1 minute more. Stir in shredded chicken, 1 cup enchilada sauce, and cilantro.

3. Place a heaping spoonful of chicken mixture on each cabbage leaf. Fold up short sides of the cabbage leaf, then roll up like a burrito and place in 9x13-inch baking dish.

4. Spoon remaining ⅓ cup enchilada sauce over enchiladas and sprinkle with both cheeses.

5. Bake until cheese is melty, about 20 minutes.

6. In a small bowl, stir together sour cream and lime juice, then drizzle over enchiladas. Garnish with cilantro before serving.

ZUCCHINI LASAGNA ROLL-UPS

TOTAL TIME
20 MIN

SERVES
10

This recipe takes some time and patience, but it's just about the prettiest "pasta" dish you'll ever see. If you have a mandoline, use it to make noodles; if you don't, practice your knife skills. 😉

6 large zucchini, sliced lengthwise into ⅛–inch thick strips

1 (16–ounce) container ricotta

½ cup freshly grated Parmesan, divided

2 large eggs

½ teaspoon garlic powder

Kosher salt

Freshly ground black pepper

1 cup marinara

1 cup shredded mozzarella

1. Preheat oven to 400°. Drain sliced zucchini on a paper towel–lined baking sheet.

2. In a small bowl, combine ricotta, ¼ cup Parmesan, eggs, and garlic powder, and season with salt and pepper.

3. Spread a thin layer of marinara on bottom of a 9x13–inch baking dish. On each slice of zucchini, spoon a thin layer of marinara, spread ricotta mixture on top, and sprinkle with mozzarella. Roll up and place in baking dish, making sure roll–ups are packed together tightly.

4. Sprinkle with remaining ¼ cup Parmesan. Bake until zucchini is tender and cheese is melty, 20 minutes.

CHEESESTEAK STUFFED PEPPERS

TOTAL TIME
45 MIN

SERVES
6

Ditch the bread (and the Cheez Whiz) and accept the fact that these mushroom and pepper "cheesesteaks" are 95% inauthentic and 100% amazing.

---

3 bell peppers, halved, cores removed
1 tablespoon extra-virgin olive oil
1 large red onion, sliced

8 ounces cremini mushrooms, sliced
Kosher salt
Freshly ground black pepper
1 pound sirloin steak, thinly sliced

2 teaspoons Italian seasoning
12 slices provolone
Freshly chopped parsley, for garnish
Crushed red pepper flakes, for garnish

---

1. Preheat oven to 350°. Place peppers in a large baking dish and bake until tender, 30 minutes.

2. Meanwhile, in a large skillet over medium-high heat, heat oil. Add onion and mushrooms and season with salt and pepper. Cook until soft, 5 minutes. Add steak and season with more salt and pepper. Cook, stirring occasionally, 3 minutes, then stir in Italian seasoning.

3. Add one slice of provolone to bottom of each pepper and top with steak mixture. Top with another piece of provolone and broil until golden, 3 minutes.

4. Garnish with parsley and red pepper flakes before serving.

UNSTUFFED CABBAGE CASSEROLE

TOTAL TIME
1 HR 35 MIN

SERVES 6

We took everything you love about traditional stuffed cabbage and turned it into a crowd-friendly casserole. You don't even need to cook the rice beforehand—it cooks in the big and bubbly bake.

Cooking spray

2 tablespoons extra-virgin olive oil

1 large onion, chopped

3 cloves garlic, minced

1 pound ground beef

2 tablespoons tomato paste

1 (14.5-ounce) can chopped tomatoes

1 cup rice

3 cups low-sodium chicken broth (or water)

1 teaspoon dried oregano

Kosher salt

Freshly ground black pepper

1 large head cabbage, roughly chopped

Freshly chopped parsley, for garnish

---

1. Preheat oven to 350° and grease a 9x13-inch baking dish with cooking spray. In a large Dutch oven or pot over medium heat, heat oil. Add onion and cook until soft, about 5 minutes. Stir in garlic and cook until fragrant, 1 minute more. Add ground beef, breaking up meat with a wooden spoon, and cook until no longer pink, about 6 minutes. Drain fat.

2. Return beef mixture to skillet. Stir in tomato paste until beef is coated, then add chopped tomatoes, rice, and 2 cups broth. Season with oregano, salt, and pepper. Bring mixture to a simmer and cook 10 minutes, stirring frequently to prevent rice from scorching. Gradually stir in cabbage and cook until slightly wilted, 5 minutes. Stir in remaining 1 cup broth.

3. Transfer mixture to prepared baking dish and cover dish with foil.

4. Bake until rice is tender, about 40 minutes.

5. Garnish with parsley before serving.

EGGPLANT LASAGNA

TOTAL TIME
1 HR 30 MIN

SERVES 4

Call it eggplant lasagna or call it eggplant parm, it doesn't matter. The only thing you'll care about is if there's enough for seconds.

---

2 medium eggplants
Kosher salt
1 tablespoon extra-virgin olive oil
3 cloves garlic, minced
1 onion, chopped

2 teaspoons dried oregano
Freshly ground black pepper
1 (25-ounce) jar marinara
1 (16-ounce) container ricotta
½ cup freshly grated Parmesan, plus more for garnish

1 large egg
¼ cup freshly chopped parsley, plus more for garnish
4 cups shredded mozzarella

---

1. Preheat oven to 400°. Cut ends of eggplants and slice thinly, about ¼-inch thick. Lay slices on a cooling rack and season with salt. Let sit for 20 minutes. Flip, season again, and let sit for another 20 minutes. Pat dry with paper towels.

2. In a large skillet over medium heat, heat oil. Sauté garlic for 1 minute, then add onions and oregano. Season with salt and pepper and cook until onions are translucent. Add marinara and cook until warmed through.

3. In a medium bowl, combine ricotta, Parmesan, egg, and parsley. Season with salt and pepper.

4. In a 9x13-inch baking dish, spread a thin layer of marinara sauce, a single layer of eggplant "noodles," a layer of ricotta mixture, then a layer of mozzarella; repeat layers. Top last layer of eggplant with marinara sauce, mozzarella, and Parmesan.

5. Cover with foil and bake for 35 minutes, then garnish with parsley and serve.

BEST-EVER SIDES

CREAMED BRUSSELS SPROUTS

TOTAL TIME
1 HR

SERVES 6

Quite possibly one of our all-time favorite sides, this lightened take on creamed spinach tastes just as good next to a big ribeye steak as it does grilled chicken breast. It's always a winner.

---

1 tablespoon extra-virgin olive oil

½ large yellow onion, chopped

3 cloves garlic, minced

2 pounds Brussels sprouts, halved and thinly sliced

1 cup Greek yogurt

½ cup mayonnaise

2 large eggs, lightly beaten

Zest of ½ lemon

½ cup shredded Fontina

½ cup freshly grated Parmesan, plus extra for serving

Kosher salt

Freshly ground black pepper

Freshly chopped parsley, for serving

Crushed red pepper flakes, for serving

---

1. Preheat oven to 375°. In a large skillet over medium heat, heat oil. Add onion and cook until soft, 5 minutes. Add garlic and cook until fragrant, 1 minute. Add Brussels sprouts and cook until tender, 7 minutes more. Remove from heat and cool slightly.

2. In a large bowl, stir together yogurt, mayo, eggs, lemon zest, and cheeses and season with salt and pepper. Fold in cooled Brussels sprouts and transfer to a 9x13-inch baking dish.

3. Bake until cheese is melty and golden, 30 to 35 minutes.

4. Garnish with parsley, Parmesan, and red pepper flakes before serving.

PRO TIP!
Buy store–bought
shaved Brussels sprouts
if you can. It'll cut back
significantly on the
prep time.

CHEESY BACON-ASPARAGUS CASSEROLE

TOTAL TIME 1 HR 25 MIN

SERVES 6

Meet spring's version of green bean casserole, with two very major upgrades—Ritz crackers (!!!) and bacon cream sauce. We repeat: bacon cream sauce.

- 6 slices bacon, cut into 1-inch pieces
- 2 cloves garlic, minced
- ¼ cup all-purpose flour
- 1½ cups whole milk
- ½ cup heavy cream

- 1 cup shredded white cheddar, divided
- 1 cup shredded Gruyère, divided
- Kosher salt
- Freshly ground black pepper

- Pinch crushed red pepper flakes
- 1 bunch asparagus, ends trimmed
- 1 cup crushed Ritz crackers

---

1. Preheat oven to 375°. In a large skillet over medium heat, cook bacon until crispy, 10 minutes. Remove from pan with a slotted spoon and drain on a paper towel–lined plate. Drain all but ¼ cup of grease from pan.

2. To same skillet, add garlic and cook until fragrant, 1 minute. Add flour and stir until golden, 2 minutes. Slowly pour in milk and cream, whisking until smooth. Let simmer until thickened, 5 minutes. Add ½ cup each of cheddar and Gruyère and stir until melted.

3. Return bacon to sauce and season with salt and pepper and red pepper flakes.

4. Place asparagus in a 9x13-inch baking pan and pour sauce over, then top with remaining ½ cup of each cheese and crushed Ritz crackers.

5. Cover with foil and bake until asparagus is tender, 20 minutes. Remove foil and bake until cheese is melty, 10 minutes more.

BEST-EVER CANDIED YAMS

TOTAL TIME

1 HR 55 MIN

SERVES
8

Once you try yams with bourbon, there's no going back. And once you make this recipe, there's no Thanksgiving without it.

3 tablespoons butter,
  plus more for pan
½ cup dark brown sugar
½ cup orange juice

1 cinnamon stick
2 tablespoons bourbon
  (optional)
Pinch nutmeg

Pinch kosher salt
5 medium sweet potatoes
  (about 3 pounds)

1. Preheat oven to 400° and butter a medium baking dish.

2. In a medium saucepan over medium heat, combine sugar, orange juice, butter, cinnamon stick, bourbon if using, nutmeg, and salt. Stir to combine and bring to a boil, then reduce to a simmer and cook until it has thickened slightly, about 10 minutes. When reduced, remove and discard cinnamon stick.

3. Meanwhile, prep potatoes: Peel potatoes and slice into ½-inch rounds, then layer in prepared baking dish. Pour thickened syrup over potatoes and cover dish with aluminum foil.

4. Bake 30 minutes, then remove foil and bake about 50 minutes to 1 hour more, basting with sauce every 15 minutes.

5. Let cool slightly before serving.

SCALLOPED ZUCCHINI

TOTAL TIME
1 HR 5 MIN

SERVES 6

While developing this recipe, we learned one very important lesson: People don't love scalloped potatoes for the potatoes themselves—it's all about the sauce and cheese, both of which are gloriously present here.

2 tablespoons butter, plus more for buttering pan

2 cloves garlic, minced

2 tablespoons all-purpose flour

1½ cups whole milk

2 cups shredded Gruyère, divided

½ cup freshly grated Parmesan

Kosher salt

Freshly ground black pepper

Pinch nutmeg

4 medium zucchini, sliced crosswise into ¼-inch coins

2 teaspoons freshly chopped thyme

Freshly chopped parsley, for garnish

1. Preheat oven to 375° and butter a medium casserole dish. In a large skillet over medium heat, melt butter. Add garlic and cook until fragrant, about 1 minute. Whisk in flour and cook until flour is golden and starts to bubble, about 1 minute more. Add milk and stir until mixture comes to a simmer. Boil until slightly thickened, about 1 minute.

2. Turn off heat and add 1 cup Gruyère and Parmesan. Stir until cheese has melted, then season with salt, pepper, and nutmeg.

3. Add a layer of zucchini to baking dish, overlapping zucchini slices. Season with salt and pepper and pour about one-third of cream mixture over zucchini. Sprinkle some of remaining Gruyère on top, then sprinkle thyme on top of cheese.

4. Make two more layers with remaining zucchini slices, cream mixture, cheese, and thyme. Bake until bubbly and golden on top, 23 to 25 minutes.

5. Garnish with parsley and serve warm.

TWICE-BAKED POTATO CASSEROLE

TOTAL TIME
2 HR 20 MIN

SERVES 8

When it comes to twice–baked potatoes, the cheesy filling is what really psychs people up. Which is why we felt justified about loading it into a big casserole dish instead of stuffing it back into a vessel that no one wants to bother with.

6 large russet potatoes
4 tablespoons butter, softened, plus more for pan
4 ounces cream cheese, softened
1 cup sour cream
1½ cups whole milk
2¾ cups shredded cheddar, divided
10 slices cooked bacon, crumbled
5 green onions, sliced
¾ teaspoon garlic powder
Kosher salt
Freshly ground black pepper

1. Preheat oven to 400°. Place potatoes directly on rack and bake until soft and easily pierced with the tip of a knife, 1 hour to 1 hour 15 minutes, depending on size. Remove from oven and let cool slightly.

2. Slice warm potatoes in half, remove flesh with a spoon, and place in a large bowl; discard skin.

3. Mash flesh and combine with butter, cream cheese, sour cream, and milk, stirring until butter and cream cheese are melted. Fold in 2 cups cheddar, three–quarters of bacon, three–quarters of chopped green onion, and garlic powder. Season with salt and pepper.

4. Brush a medium baking dish with butter and scrape potato mixture into dish. Sprinkle with remaining ¾ cup cheddar cheese and bake until cheese is melty, about 20 minutes. Turn oven to broil and broil until golden, about 2 minutes. Let cool 10 minutes.

5. Top with remaining bacon and green onions.

PRO TIP!

Make sure to thoroughly dry the blanched cauliflower before layering it into the sauce. Otherwise, you'll end up with a watery mess!

CAULIFLOWER AU GRATIN

TOTAL TIME
55 MIN

SERVES 6

Sometimes choosing to eat low-carb means devouring a cheesy cauliflower au gratin. Life without potatoes may be easier than you think.

2 tablespoons butter, plus more for pan
1 large head cauliflower, cut into florets
2 cloves garlic, minced
2 tablespoons all-purpose flour

1½ cups whole milk
2 cups shredded Gruyère, divided
½ cup freshly grated Parmesan

2 teaspoons freshly chopped thyme
Kosher salt
Freshly ground black pepper
Freshly chopped parsley, for garnish

1. Preheat oven to 375° and butter a medium casserole dish. In a large pot of boiling salted water, cook cauliflower for 3 minutes. Use a slotted spoon to transfer to a bowl of ice water to cool. Drain and pat dry.

2. In a large skillet over medium heat, melt butter. Add garlic and cook until fragrant, about 1 minute. Whisk in flour and cook until flour is golden and starts to bubble, about 1 minute more. Add milk slowly and stir until mixture comes to a simmer. Boil until slightly thickened, about 1 minute.

3. Turn off heat and add 1 cup Gruyère, Parmesan, and thyme. Stir until cheese has melted, then season with salt and pepper.

4. Add about half of cauliflower to prepared pan, then pour in half of cream mixture. Repeat with remaining cauliflower and cream, then top with remaining 1 cup of Gruyère.

5. Bake until bubbly and golden on top, about 25 minutes. Garnish with parsley and serve warm.

SWEET NOODLE KUGEL

TOTAL TIME

1 HR 20 MIN

MAKES 8

Not too sweet and with a hint of cinnamon, this kugel recipe is *the* one. Don't make it if you don't want endless praise and compliments.

Butter, for pan
1 (16-ounce) package wide egg noodles
5 large eggs

½ cup butter, melted
1 (16-ounce) container sour cream

1 (8-ounce) container cottage cheese
¾ cup sugar
½ teaspoon cinnamon

1. Preheat oven to 350° and butter a 9x13-inch baking dish. In a large pot of boiling water, cook pasta until al dente, 5 minutes. Drain.

2. In a large bowl, mix together eggs, butter, sour cream, cottage cheese, sugar, and cinnamon, then stir in noodles. Pour into prepared dish and bake until set, 1 hour. Cover with aluminum foil if top starts to get too dark.

YELLOW SQUASH CASSEROLE

TOTAL TIME
40 MIN

SERVES
6

It's nothing fancy, but it's everything. Believe us when we say that no one is above a cheesy, sour cream and mayo casserole that gets topped with two sleeves of Ritz crackers.

---

4 tablespoons butter, divided
2 pounds yellow squash,
  sliced into ½–inch coins
1 onion, chopped
2 cloves garlic, minced

Kosher salt
Freshly ground black pepper
¼ teaspoon cayenne pepper
2 large eggs
½ cup sour cream

¼ cup mayonnaise
1½ cups shredded cheddar
1 cup freshly grated Parmesan
2 sleeves Ritz crackers,
  crushed

---

1. Preheat oven to 350° and lightly grease a medium casserole dish.

2. In a large skillet over medium heat, melt 2 tablespoons butter. Add the squash and onion and cook, stirring often, until the squash is tender, about 8 minutes. Stir in garlic and season with salt, pepper, and cayenne pepper. Transfer mixture to a colander set over a bowl and let drain for 5 minutes. Discard liquid.

3. In a large bowl, whisk together eggs, sour cream, and mayonnaise. Stir in cheddar and Parmesan and season mixture with salt and pepper. Gently fold in squash mixture, then transfer mixture to the prepared baking dish.

4. Melt remaining 2 tablespoons of butter and toss with Ritz crackers. Sprinkle cracker mixture over casserole. Bake until golden and bubbly, about 20 minutes.

LOADED SCALLOPED POTATOES

TOTAL TIME
1 HR 40 MIN

SERVES
8

Creamy potatoes + crispy, smoky bacon + cheese = a no-brainer. Because cheddar melts and mingles with the cream sauce while the casserole bakes, it gives off major mac and cheese sauce vibes.

---

6 slices bacon, chopped into 1-inch pieces
3 tablespoons butter
3 garlic cloves, minced
3 tablespoons all-purpose flour

2 cups heavy cream
1 cup low-sodium chicken broth
Kosher salt
Freshly ground black pepper

2 pounds russet potatoes, rinsed and scrubbed clean
2 cups shredded cheddar
Finely chopped chives, for garnish

---

1. Preheat oven to 400°. In a large skillet over medium heat, cook bacon until crispy, about 8 minutes. Drain on paper towels.

2. In another large skillet over medium heat, melt butter. Add garlic and cook until fragrant, about 1 minute. Stir in flour and cook for another minute. Whisk in cream and chicken broth and season with salt and pepper. Simmer until thickened slightly, about 5 minutes. Remove from heat.

3. Peel potatoes and thinly slice each potato crosswise into thin coins. (A mandoline would work great here.)

4. Spoon a thin layer of sauce into bottom of a large casserole dish. Add a single layer of potatoes on top. Spoon more sauce over potatoes and top with cheese and bacon. Repeat three to four times, or until casserole dish is mostly full.

5. Bake until sauce is bubbly and potatoes are very tender, about 1 hour 15 minutes. Let rest for at least 15 minutes before serving.

6. Garnish with chives before serving.

PRO TIP!

Bake it longer than you think you need to. When you test a potato with a paring knife, you want it to almost fall apart from being so soft.

SAUSAGE STUFFING

TOTAL TIME
40 MIN

SERVES
6

We love that this gets super toasty on the outside and remains nice and soft in the middle. But if everyone in the fam is into verging–on–soggy stuffing (seriously, it's a thing!), we recommend covering the casserole dish with aluminum foil while baking.

- 1 large boule (or 2 baguettes)
- 6 tablespoons butter, divided, plus more for baking dish
- 4 stalks celery, thinly sliced
- 1 large onion, chopped
- 2 cloves garlic, minced
- 1 tablespoon freshly chopped sage
- 2 teaspoons fresh thyme leaves
- 2 teaspoons freshly chopped rosemary
- Kosher salt
- Freshly ground black pepper
- 1 tablespoon freshly chopped parsley, plus more for garnish
- 1 pound sausage, casings removed
- 1½ cups low–sodium chicken broth
- ½ cup dried cranberries

---

1. Tear or slice bread into cubes and leave out overnight to dry. (Alternately, place bread on baking sheets and bake at 200° for 20 minutes.)

2. Preheat oven to 350° and butter a large baking dish. In a large skillet over medium heat, melt 3 tablespoons butter. Add onion and celery and cook until soft and fragrant, 8 minutes. Stir in garlic, sage, thyme, and rosemary and cook until fragrant, 1 minute more. Season with salt and pepper. Stir in remaining 3 tablespoons butter and parsley. Toss with bread in a large bowl.

3. In same skillet over medium–high heat, cook sausage until seared and cooked through, about 10 minutes, stirring often.

4. Add cooked sausage, broth, and cranberries to bread mixture. Transfer mixture to prepared baking dish and cover with foil. Bake until cooked through, 45 minutes, then remove foil and cook until bread is golden, 15 minutes more. Garnish with more parsley and serve.

7

AMAZING
DESSERTS

PEANUT BUTTER CAKE

TOTAL TIME
1 HR

SERVES 10

Here's the deal: If you think we went too far with this recipe, you're not a true peanut butter lover.

FOR THE CAKE
Cooking spray
2½ cups all–purpose flour
2 teaspoons baking powder
½ teaspoon kosher salt
¾ cup (1½ sticks) butter, softened
1 cup packed brown sugar
½ cup granulated sugar
3 large eggs
¾ cup peanut butter
½ cup sour cream
1 tablespoon pure vanilla extract
¾ cup whole milk

FOR THE FROSTING
1 (8–ounce) block cream cheese, softened
4 tablespoons butter, softened
1¼ cups peanut butter
2 cups powdered sugar
1 teaspoon pure vanilla extract
Pinch kosher salt
2 tablespoons milk

FOR TOPPING
½ cup peanut butter, melted
½ cup chopped mini Reese's
¼ cup mini chocolate chips

1. Preheat oven to 350° and grease a 9x13–inch baking pan with cooking spray. In a large bowl, whisk together flour, baking powder, and salt.

2. In another large bowl using a hand mixer, beat together butter and sugars until light and fluffy. Add eggs, one at a time, then add peanut butter, sour cream, and vanilla, beating until smooth.

3. Add half of dry ingredients, beating until just combined. Pour in milk and mix until fully incorporated, then add remaining dry ingredients and mix until just combined.

4. Pour batter into prepared pan and smooth top. Bake until a toothpick inserted into middle comes out clean, 35 minutes. Let cool completely.

5. Make frosting: In a large bowl using a hand mixer, beat cream cheese and butter until no lumps remain. Add peanut butter and beat until light and fluffy. Add powdered sugar, vanilla, and salt and mix until well combined. Add milk and mix until fully incorporated.

6. Frost cake, then drizzle with melted peanut butter and top with mini Reese's and chocolate chips.

PEACH DUMP CAKE

TOTAL TIME
1 HR 5 MIN

SERVES 8

Dump cakes never cease to amaze us. If you're new to (or afraid of) baking, give this recipe a try. It's basically foolproof.

Cooking spray
2 (15–ounce) cans sliced
   peaches in syrup

1 teaspoon ground cinnamon
1 box yellow cake mix

¾ cup (1½ sticks) butter,
   cut into small cubes
Ice cream, for serving

1. Preheat oven to 350° and grease a medium baking dish with cooking spray. Combine peaches and cinnamon in prepared baking dish and stir to combine.

2. Pour cake mix over peaches in an even layer. Dot all over with butter and bake until fruit is bubbly and cake is cooked through, 50 to 55 minutes. Serve with ice cream.

APPLE COBBLER

TOTAL TIME
1 HR 30 MIN

SERVES **6**

When life gives you apples, you make cobbler. The same goes for peaches and blueberries. This buttery biscuit topping pairs beautifully with both.

FOR THE APPLES
6 apples, cored and sliced
¼ cup packed brown sugar
2 teaspoons ground cinnamon
½ teaspoon kosher salt
Juice of ½ lemon

FOR THE COBBLER
2 cups all-purpose flour
½ cup granulated sugar
2 teaspoons baking powder
½ teaspoon kosher salt
½ cup (1 stick) butter, cold, cut into ½-inch cubes

½ cup heavy cream
1 large egg, beaten
Egg wash, for brushing
Coarse sugar, for sprinkling

---

1. Preheat oven to 350°. In a large bowl, combine apples, brown sugar, cinnamon, salt, and lemon juice. Let apples macerate for 15 minutes.

2. In another large bowl, whisk together flour, sugar, baking powder, and salt. Incorporate butter into flour mixture until it resembles coarse crumbs, then stir in heavy cream and egg.

3. Pour apples into a large baking dish and top with dollops of dough. Brush dough with egg wash and sprinkle with coarse sugar. Bake until golden brown and bubbling, 1 hour. Let rest 10 minutes before serving.

PEANUT BUTTER DESSERT LASAGNA

TOTAL TIME
6 HR 40 MIN

SERVES 8

Layered with Nutter Butters, peanut butter, vanilla pudding, whipped cream, and Butterfingers, this dessert is not for the faint of heart. It is, however, for true peanut butter fans.

1½ cups heavy cream
½ cup powdered sugar
1 (3.4–ounce) package vanilla instant pudding mix, plus ingredients called for on box

1 (16–ounce) package Nutter Butters
1 (16.3–ounce) jar peanut butter, melted

3 King Size Butterfingers, roughly chopped
½ cup semisweet chocolate chips, melted

1. Make whipped cream: Using a stand mixer with whisk attachment or hand beaters, beat cream and sugar until medium peaks form, about 3 minutes. Set aside.

2. Prepare pudding according to package directions.

3. In an 8x8–inch baking dish, spread a thin layer of whipped cream. Top with a layer of Nutter Butters and a layer of melted peanut butter, spreading to completely cover cookies. Top with half of prepared vanilla pudding, spreading into an even layer, then half of remaining whipped cream in an even layer. Top with half of crushed Butterfingers and drizzle with more melted peanut butter. Repeat layering with remaining Nutter Butters, pudding, whipped cream, and crushed Butterfingers.

4. Cover loosely with plastic wrap and refrigerate until cookies are soft, 6 hours and up to overnight.

5. Drizzle with remaining melted peanut butter and melted chocolate, then slice and serve.

MINT CHIP LASAGNA

TOTAL TIME
4 HR 50 MIN

SERVES 12

The definition of a perfect bite: buttery Oreo crust, peppermint cheesecake, double chocolate pudding, whipped cream, chocolate shavings, *and* mini chocolate chips. We dare you to try to think of something better.

FOR THE CRUST

1 package mint Oreos, finely crushed

5 tablespoons melted butter

FOR THE CHEESECAKE LAYER

2 (8-ounce) blocks cream cheese, softened

1 cup powdered sugar

1 teaspoon mint extract

1 cup whipped cream

Green food coloring

FOR THE PUDDING LAYER

2 (3.4-ounce) packages instant chocolate pudding

3 cups whole milk

½ cup mini chocolate chips

FOR THE TOPPING

2 cups whipped cream

¼ cup chocolate shavings

¼ cup mini chocolate chips

1. In a medium bowl, combine crushed Oreos and butter. Press into a 9x13-inch baking dish.

2. Make cheesecake layer: In another large bowl, using a hand mixer, beat cream cheese and powdered sugar until no lumps remain, then beat in mint extract. Fold in whipped cream until incorporated. Add green food coloring until desired color is reached. Pour cheesecake layer over crust and smooth top with an offset spatula. Refrigerate while making the next layer.

3. Make pudding layer: In a large bowl, whisk together pudding mix and milk until thickened, then fold in mini chocolate chips. Pour pudding over cheesecake layer and smooth top.

4. Spread whipped cream over pudding layer and top with chocolate shavings and mini chocolate chips. Refrigerate until well chilled, at least 4 hours and up to overnight.

PRO TIP!
Mint Oreos are preferred, but if you already have the classic kind on hand, feel free to swap them in instead.

OREO DIRT CAKE

TOTAL TIME
3 HR
40 MIN

SERVES
10

Because people really just want the dirt cake they grew up with, we kept things pretty classic. To really drive home the dirt effect, top the whole cake with gummy worms.

1 (14.3–ounce) package Oreos
4 tablespoons melted butter
1 (3.4–oz) box instant vanilla pudding
1½ cups cold milk
1 (8–ounce) block cream cheese, softened
½ cup powdered sugar
1 cup heavy cream

1. In a food processor, finely crush Oreos. In a large bowl, add all but ¾ cup crushed Oreos and melted butter and stir until mixture starts to hold together. Pour mixture into 9x9–inch baking dish and pack into an even layer.

2. In a medium bowl, whisk together pudding mix and milk until thickened, then refrigerate for 10 minutes to firm up.

3. In a large bowl using a hand mixer, beat cream cheese and powdered sugar together until no lumps remain.

4. In another large bowl, beat cream until stiff peaks form. Fold pudding into cream cheese mixture, then fold in whipped cream until just combined. Pour mixture over Oreo crust and smooth with an offset spatula. Top with reserved ¾ cup crushed Oreos.

5. Refrigerate until well chilled, at least 3 hours and up to overnight.

SAMOA DESSERT LASAGNA

TOTAL TIME
2 HR 25 MIN

SERVES 12

You don't make this dessert lasagna if you have a box of Girl Scout cookies. You make it when you're desperately craving Samoas.

FOR THE CRUST
1½ cups crushed Nilla wafers
½ cup toasted shredded coconut
6 tablespoons melted butter

FOR THE CARAMEL LAYER
1 (10.4-ounce) jar caramel

FOR THE CHOCOLATE LAYER
2 (3.9-ounce) boxes instant chocolate pudding
2 cups cold milk

FOR THE CREAM CHEESE LAYER
2 cups heavy cream
1 (8-ounce) block cream cheese, softened
½ cup powdered sugar

FOR TOPPING
1 cup toasted, sweetened coconut flakes
½ cup chocolate chips, melted
Caramel, warmed, for drizzling

1. Preheat oven to 350°. In a medium bowl, combine crushed Nillas, coconut, and melted butter. Press into bottom of a 9x13-inch baking dish and bake until golden, 10 to 12 minutes. Let cool.

2. Pour caramel over cooled crust and spread into an even layer.

3. In another medium bowl, combine pudding mix and milk; whisk until thickened. Pour over caramel and smooth into an even layer.

4. In a large bowl, beat heavy cream into stiff peaks. In a medium bowl, beat cream cheese and powdered sugar until no lumps remain, then fold in whipped cream. Spoon mixture over pudding and smooth into an even layer. Refrigerate until well chilled, at least 2 hours.

5. When ready to serve, top with toasted coconut and drizzle with melted chocolate and caramel.

BANANA PUDDING POKE CAKE

TOTAL TIME
1 HR

SERVES
12

True or false: you can transform any dessert into a poke cake. (The answer is true. Very, very true.)

Cooking spray
1 (16.5-ounce) box yellow cake mix, plus ingredients called for on box

2 (3.4-ounce) boxes vanilla pudding mix
3 cups whole milk
2 cups heavy cream
2 tablespoons granulated sugar

1 teaspoon pure vanilla extract
3 bananas, thinly sliced
10 Nilla wafers, crushed

---

1. Preheat oven to 350° and grease a 9x13-inch baking pan with cooking spray. Prepare yellow cake mix according to box instructions. Pour batter into prepared pan and bake until a toothpick inserted in the middle comes out clean, about 25 minutes. Let cool completely.

2. Prepare pudding: In a small bowl, whisk together pudding mix and milk until thickened.

3. Make whipped cream: In another large bowl using a hand mixer, beat cream, sugar, and vanilla until stiff peaks form.

4. Poke cooled cake all over with bottom of a wooden spoon. Spread pudding mixture on cake, then top with a layer of banana slices. Spread whipped cream on top.

5. Sprinkle all over with crushed Nilla wafers and garnish with more bananas.

OREOGASM POKE CAKE

TOTAL TIME
45 MIN

SERVES 10

This easy chocolate poke cake is so good, it's almost NSFW.

Cooking spray
1 (16.5–ounce) box chocolate cake mix, plus ingredients called for on box
1½ cups marshmallow crème

1 tablespoon water
½ cup finely ground Oreos
2 cups heavy cream
½ cup powdered sugar
½ teaspoon kosher salt

1 cup crushed Oreos, divided
6 Oreos, halved
Chocolate fudge sauce, for drizzling

---

1. Preheat oven to 350° and grease a 9x13–inch pan with cooking spray. Prepare chocolate cake mix according to box instructions and bake until a toothpick inserted in the center comes out clean, about 25 minutes. Let cool completely.

2. In a small bowl, combine marshmallow crème and water, then microwave until melty, 20 seconds. Stir until smooth, then fold in ground Oreos.

3. Poke cake all over with bottom of a wooden spoon. Pour marshmallow mixture all over poke holes.

4. Make whipped cream: In a large bowl using a hand mixer, beat heavy cream, powdered sugar, and salt until medium peaks form. Fold in ½ cup crushed Oreos.

5. Spread whipped cream all over cake with an offset spatula and sprinkle with remaining ½ cup crushed Oreos. Top with halved Oreos and drizzle with chocolate fudge sauce before serving.

DEATH BY CHOCOLATE POKE CAKE

TOTAL TIME
1 HR

SERVES
12

Calling all chocoholics! This insanely decadent poke cake is almost impossible not to eat straight from the pan. The condensed milk + melted chocolate filling is killer.

FOR THE CAKE

Cooking spray
Cocoa powder
1 box chocolate cake mix, plus
ingredients called for on box
1 (14-ounce) can sweetened
condensed milk
1 cup semisweet chocolate chips,
melted
Chocolate shavings, for garnish

FOR THE FROSTING

1 cup butter, softened
2½ cups powdered sugar
¾ cup cocoa powder
2 teaspoons pure vanilla extract
Pinch kosher salt
¼ cup heavy cream, plus more
if necessary

1. Make cake: Preheat oven to 350° and grease a 9x13-inch pan with cooking spray and dust with cocoa powder. Prepare chocolate cake mix according to package directions and bake until a toothpick inserted in center comes out clean, 25 to 30 minutes. Let cool completely.

2. Poke cake all over with the handle of a wooden spoon. In a small bowl, mix together sweetened condensed milk and melted chocolate. Pour mixture into holes.

3. Make frosting: In a large bowl using a hand mixer, beat butter, powdered sugar, cocoa powder, vanilla, and salt. Beat in heavy cream, adding more by tablespoonful until consistency is creamy but can hold peaks.

4. Spread frosting over cake with an offset spatula and sprinkle with chocolate shavings.

RASPBERRY PEACH UPSIDE-DOWN CAKE

TOTAL TIME
1 HR 30 MIN

SERVES 10

One bite of the caramelized peach and raspberry topping, and this cake will haunt your dreams.

Cooking spray
½ cup (1 stick) melted butter
   plus ½ cup (1 stick)
   softened butter, divided
2 cups granulated sugar,
   divided
2 large ripe peaches, sliced

3 teaspoons cornstarch,
   divided
2 (6-ounce) packages
   raspberries
2⅔ cups all-purpose flour
2 teaspoons baking powder
1 teaspoon kosher salt

½ cup packed brown sugar
2 large eggs
½ cup sour cream
1 teaspoon pure vanilla extract
½ cup whole milk

---

1. Preheat oven to 350° and line a 9x13-inch baking pan with parchment and grease with cooking spray. In a medium bowl, stir together melted butter and 1 cup sugar. Spread in an even layer in prepared pan. In another medium bowl, toss peaches with 1 teaspoon cornstarch. In a small bowl, toss raspberries with remaining 2 teaspoons cornstarch. Overlap peaches to make a stripe, then add an even layer of raspberries to make another stripe. Repeat two more times.

2. In a small bowl, whisk together flour, baking powder, and salt. In another large bowl using a hand mixer, beat softened butter with remaining sugars until light and fluffy. Beat in eggs, sour cream, and vanilla, then slowly beat in flour mixture and milk until just combined. Pour over fruit and smooth.

3. Bake until cake is golden evenly across top, sides of cake begin to pull away from pan, and a toothpick comes out clean, about 50 minutes.

4. Remove cake from oven, let cool 15 minutes, then flip cake upside-down onto a large serving platter or cutting board. Let rest 30 seconds, then carefully remove pan. Let cake cool completely before slicing and serving.

PUMPKIN DUMP CAKE

TOTAL TIME
1 HR 30 MIN

SERVES
8

As soon as August hits, we're struck with pumpkin fever. And this is one of the first recipes we make. Equal parts pumpkin pie filling and yellow cake, it's the best of both worlds.

Cooking spray

1 (29-ounce) can pumpkin purée

1 (12-ounce) can evaporated milk

1 cup dark brown sugar

3 large eggs

3 teaspoons pumpkin pie spice

1 box yellow cake mix

1 cup chopped pecans

1 cup (2 sticks) butter, sliced

Whipped cream, for serving

---

1. Preheat the oven to 350° and grease a 9x13-inch baking dish with cooking spray.

2. In a large bowl, whisk together pumpkin, evaporated milk, brown sugar, eggs, and pumpkin pie spice. Pour into prepared pan.

3. In a medium bowl, stir cake mix and pecans together, then sprinkle evenly over pumpkin mixture. Place pats of butter evenly on top.

4. Bake until cake is set and edges are crisp, about 50 minutes. Let cool completely, then cut into squares and top with whipped cream.

CHAPTER

8

BRUNCH FAVORITES

BREAKFAST STRATA

TOTAL TIME
1 HR 20 MIN

SERVES
8

The beauty of this casserole is its flexibility. Chorizo would be an amazing substitute for the sausage, half-and-half would be an upgrade from milk, and any type of melty cheese would work. Got kale? Use it and leave out the spinach. Not a fan of mushrooms? Skip them!

1 tablespoon butter

1 pound sweet Italian sausage, casings removed

10 large eggs

2 cups whole milk

Kosher salt

Freshly ground black pepper

4 cups cubed bread

1½ cups shredded Fontina, divided

1 cup frozen spinach, defrosted, drained and chopped

1 cup sliced cremini mushrooms

1 cup halved grape tomatoes

Torn basil, for garnish

1. Preheat oven to 350° and grease a 9x13-inch baking dish with butter. In a large skillet over medium-high heat, add sausage and cook, breaking up large pieces with a spoon, until golden, about 7 minutes. Remove from heat and let cool.

2. In a large bowl, whisk together eggs and milk and season with salt and pepper. Gently fold in bread, 1 cup cheese, spinach, mushrooms, tomatoes, and cooked sausage.

3. Pour mixture into prepared baking dish. Top with remaining ½ cup cheese and bake 50 to 55 minutes, until cheese is golden and no liquid remains. Garnish with basil before serving.

CROISSANT BAKE

TOTAL TIME
1 HR **30** MIN

SERVES
8

The contrast between the crispy, flaky edges of the croissant and the soft, cheesy middle is reminiscent of both stuffing and bread pudding. If you're able, assemble everything the night before and bake it the next morning. Just try to catch some zzz's. (We know it can be hard to sleep when a cheesy bacon, egg, and cheese casserole is waiting for you.)

6 large croissants, quartered

6 slices bacon

8 large eggs

3 cups milk (preferably whole)

1 cup heavy cream

2 tablespoons finely chopped chives

2 teaspoons freshly chopped thyme leaves

Kosher salt

Freshly ground black pepper

Pinch cayenne pepper

1 cup shredded Gruyère, divided

1 cup shredded mozzarella, divided

Butter, for baking dish

1. Preheat oven to 450°. Spread croissants on a large baking sheet cut-side up and bake until golden, 6 minutes.

2. Meanwhile, in a large skillet over medium heat, cook bacon until crispy, about 8 minutes. Drain on a paper towel-lined plate, then chop into bite-size pieces.

3. In a large bowl, whisk together eggs, milk, heavy cream, chives, and thyme. Season with salt, pepper, and cayenne, then stir in about ¾ cup each Gruyère and mozzarella.

4. Lightly butter a 9x13-inch baking dish. Combine croissants and cooked bacon in baking dish, then pour egg mixture on top, making sure each piece of croissant is coated. (If you have time, refrigerate 30 minutes or up to overnight.)

5. When ready to bake, preheat oven to 350°. Top casserole with remaining ¼ cup of each cheese and bake until golden, about 45 minutes.

CINNAMON ROLL BAKED OATMEAL

TOTAL TIME
1 HR 15 MIN

SERVES 12

Just because oats are healthy doesn't mean they can't be fun. And just because these oats taste like a cinnamon roll doesn't mean they're not healthy. Think about it. 😉

FOR THE OATS
1 tablespoon butter, for pan
5 cups rolled oats
1⅓ cups toasted walnuts, roughly chopped, divided
1 tablespoon ground cinnamon
3 teaspoons baking powder

1 teaspoon kosher salt
4½ cups whole milk
½ cup heavy cream
½ cup maple syrup
2 eggs, lightly beaten
2 teaspoons pure vanilla extract

FOR THE FROSTING
⅓ cup butter, softened
4 ounces cream cheese, softened
1 cup powdered sugar
2 tablespoons heavy cream

1. Preheat oven to 375° and butter a 9x13–inch baking dish. In a large bowl, stir together oats, 1 cup walnuts, cinnamon, baking powder, and kosher salt.

2. In another large bowl, whisk together milk, heavy cream, maple syrup, eggs, and vanilla. Pour dry ingredients into prepared pan, then pour wet ingredients over them. Stir to ensure there are no dry spots. Bake until top is golden and no liquid remains, 40 to 45 minutes.

3. Meanwhile, make frosting: In a large bowl, whisk together butter and cream cheese until light and fluffy. Add powdered sugar and beat until smooth. Gradually add heavy cream to loosen.

4. Let oatmeal cool, 10 minutes. Cut into squares and serve with a drizzle of frosting and a sprinkle of toasted walnuts.

SHAKSHUKA

TOTAL TIME
45 MIN

SERVES 8

By far the easiest way to impress your friends, shakshuka is the optimal brunch dish. Though the harissa is technically optional, we can't recommend it enough. It tastes amazing in eggs, pasta, hummus, and burgers. Pretty much anything!

2 tablespoons extra-virgin olive oil

1 large onion, sliced

2 red bell peppers, sliced

3 cloves garlic, minced

2 (28-ounce) cans crushed tomatoes

1 (14.5-ounce) can diced tomatoes

1 tablespoon harissa (optional)

2 teaspoons ground cumin

1 teaspoon paprika

½ teaspoon ground coriander

½ teaspoon crushed red pepper flakes

Kosher salt

Freshly ground black pepper

8 large eggs

½ cup crumbled feta

Freshly chopped parsley, for garnish

Sliced bread, for serving

1. Preheat oven to 375°. In a large skillet over medium heat, heat oil. Add onion and cook, stirring occasionally, until caramelized, 20 minutes. Add bell peppers and cook until soft, 5 minutes, then add garlic and cook until fragrant, 1 minute more. Add crushed and diced tomatoes, harissa (if using), and spices and season with salt and pepper. Simmer 10 minutes.

2. Transfer sauce to a 9x13-inch baking pan. Make 8 wells in sauce, then crack an egg into each and season with salt and pepper. Cover with foil and bake until egg whites are just set, 12 to 15 minutes.

3. Top with feta and parsley and serve warm with bread.

FRENCH TOAST CASSEROLE

TOTAL TIME
2 HR **45** MIN

SERVES
8

French toast casserole > French toast, when it means you can enjoy a mimosa (or two) with friends while the casserole comes together in the oven.

6 large eggs
1⅔ cups whole milk
1 cup heavy cream
¾ cup packed brown sugar
1 teaspoon ground cinnamon
1 teaspoon pure vanilla extract
½ teaspoon kosher salt
1 loaf white bread, preferably day-old
¼ cup sliced almonds
½ cup powdered sugar, for serving
Fresh berries, for serving (optional)

1. In a large bowl, whisk together eggs, milk, heavy cream, sugar, cinnamon, vanilla, and salt.

2. Dunk each bread slice in the egg mixture for 4 seconds, flipping once, then arrange them in a 9x13-inch baking dish in an even layer, each slice slightly overlapping the last. Pour any remaining egg mixture over bread. Cover and refrigerate, 2 hours, or up to overnight.

3. Preheat oven to 375°. Sprinkle almonds over French toast and bake in oven until tops of bread are golden and crunchy, about 35 minutes.

4. Serve topped with powdered sugar and berries.

CHICKEN & WAFFLE CASSEROLE

TOTAL TIME

1 HR 30 MIN

SERVES 8

Tbh, turning chicken and waffles into a casserole was very controversial. But we proudly stand behind our decision and have zero regrets.

---

10 toaster waffles

1 (25–ounce) package frozen breaded chicken tenders

8 large eggs

¾ cup milk

¼ cup maple syrup, plus more for serving

2 tablespoons melted butter

Kosher salt

Freshly ground black pepper

---

1. Preheat oven to 400°. Place waffles and chicken on two large baking sheets. Bake waffles until golden and crispy, 15 minutes. Continue baking chicken until warmed through and crispy, 30 minutes total. Let cool slightly, then cut both into large chunks.

2. In a large bowl, whisk together eggs, milk, maple syrup, and melted butter. Season with salt and pepper.

3. In a 9x13–inch baking dish, layer waffles and breaded chicken and pour egg mixture over top. Bake until golden and set, 1 hour.

4. Serve warm with maple syrup.

CLASSIC CINNAMON ROLLS

TOTAL TIME
3 HR 25 MIN

SERVES
12

IT'S SO FLUFFYYYY! If you're looking for ~*the*~ perfect cinnamon roll, your search is over. This is it.

FOR THE DOUGH
Cooking spray

1 cup warm whole milk

2 large eggs, at room temperature

5 tablespoons butter, softened

4½ cups all-purpose flour, plus more for surface

2 teaspoons kosher salt

½ cup granulated sugar

2½ teaspoons instant yeast or active dry yeast

¼ teaspoon baking soda

FOR THE FILLING
½ cup (1 stick) butter, softened

1 cup packed brown sugar

2 tablespoons ground cinnamon

½ teaspoon ground nutmeg

½ teaspoon kosher salt

1. Lightly grease a large bowl with cooking spray. In a separate large bowl or in the bowl of a stand mixer using a dough hook, mix together milk and yeast until yeast is mostly dissolved. Add in all remaining dough ingredients on low speed. Continue mixing on medium-high speed until a smooth, soft dough forms and starts to pull away from the sides of the bowl, 15 to 18 minutes. Transfer to prepared bowl. Cover with a kitchen towel and let rise until almost doubled, 1½ to 2 hours.

2. Meanwhile, make filling: In a large bowl using a hand mixer, beat all filling ingredients until light and fluffy, 3 to 4 minutes.

3. Preheat oven to 400° and grease a 9x13-inch pan with cooking spray. Turn dough onto a lightly floured surface and dust with more flour. Roll out into a large square, about 18x18 inches. Spread filling to edges, then roll dough into a log and cut into 12 evenly sized pieces about 1½-inch wide.

4. Place rolls cut-side up in prepared baking pan. Cover and let rise again until almost doubled, 30 minutes. Bake until golden, 18 to 20 minutes.

5. Top cinnamon rolls with frosting (opposite).

FROST IT UP!

6 ounces cream cheese, softened
½ cup butter, softened
1½ cups powdered sugar
1 teaspoon pure vanilla extract
¼ cup heavy cream

In a large bowl using a hand mixer, beat cream cheese and butter until light and fluffy. Add powdered sugar and vanilla and beat until smooth. Gradually add heavy cream until icing reaches desired consistency.

CLASSIC COFFEE CAKE

TOTAL TIME
1 HR
40 MIN

SERVES
12

We judge every coffee cake by its streusel. Ours strikes just the right balance between buttery, crumbly, and crunchy. It took us many coffee cake tests to get there, but someone had to do it.

FOR THE CAKE

¾ cup (1½ sticks) unsalted butter, softened to room temperature

1¼ cups granulated sugar

¼ cup brown sugar

3 large eggs

1¼ cups sour cream

1 teaspoon pure vanilla extract

2¼ cups all-purpose flour

¼ cup cornstarch

2 teaspoons baking powder

½ teaspoon baking soda

1 teaspoon kosher salt

FOR THE STREUSEL

½ cup packed light brown sugar

1 cup all-purpose flour

1½ teaspoons ground cinnamon

Pinch nutmeg (optional)

Pinch kosher salt

6 tablespoons butter, melted

¾ cup toasted pecans, chopped

1. Preheat oven to 350° and line a 9x13-inch pan with parchment paper. In a large bowl using a hand mixer, cream butter and sugars together until light and fluffy, 3 to 4 minutes. Add eggs, one at a time, then beat in sour cream and vanilla until just combined.

2. In another large bowl, whisk together flour, cornstarch, baking powder, baking soda, and salt. Slowly add dry ingredients into wet ingredients and beat until just incorporated.

3. Make streusel: In a medium bowl, whisk together brown sugar, flour, cinnamon, nutmeg if using, and salt. Stir in butter and pecans.

4. Add half of batter into prepared baking pan and spread in an even layer. Top with half of streusel, then add remaining batter and spread to edges of pan. Top with remaining streusel and bake until a toothpick inserted into center comes out clean, 50 to 55 minutes.

EVERYTHING BAGEL CASSEROLE

TOTAL TIME
1 HR 20 MIN

SERVES
8

You don't need New York bagels to make this dreamy breakfast bake. Cheese, eggs, and everything seasoning can transform even the blandest of grocery store bagels into something spectacular.

Cooking spray
4 everything bagels, roughly chopped
1½ cups shredded white cheddar
1½ cups halved cherry tomatoes

1 (8-ounce) block cream cheese, cut into ½-inch cubes
½ red onion, thinly sliced
8 large eggs
2½ cups milk
2 green onions, sliced, plus more for garnish
Kosher salt

Freshly ground black pepper
Pinch cayenne pepper
1 teaspoon poppy seeds
1 teaspoon dried minced onion
1 teaspoon sesame seeds
1 teaspoon dried garlic
1 teaspoon coarse salt

---

1. Preheat oven to 350° and grease a 9x13-inch baking dish with cooking spray. Scatter half of bagel pieces in prepared pan, then top with half of cheddar, tomatoes, cream cheese, and red onion. Repeat.

2. In a large bowl, whisk together eggs, milk, and green onions. Season with salt, pepper, and cayenne. Pour mixture over bagels, making sure each piece is coated.

3. Sprinkle seasonings over casserole, then cover with foil and bake 45 minutes. Remove foil and bake until golden and cooked through, about 25 minutes more. Let cool 30 minutes.

4. Garnish with green onions before serving.

BISCUITS & GRAVY BAKE

TOTAL TIME
30 MIN

SERVES
8

For anyone who's ever (1) felt that biscuits and gravy needed more gravy and (2) said gravy needed more pepper. We hear you, and we're here for you with this extra-peppery biscuits and gravy casserole.

Cooking spray
2 (16-ounce) cans refrigerated
   biscuits
2 pounds hot Italian sausage,
   casings removed

3 tablespoons all-purpose
   flour
2½ cups milk
Kosher salt
Freshly ground black pepper

Pinch cayenne pepper
2 tablespoons melted butter
Freshly chopped chives,
   for garnish

1. Preheat oven to 375° and grease a 9x13-inch baking dish with cooking spray. Cut biscuits into quarters and add half to prepared pan. Bake until golden, 12 to 15 minutes.

2. Meanwhile make gravy: In a large skillet over medium heat, cook sausage, breaking up meat with a wooden spoon, until no longer pink, about 6 minutes. Add flour and cook 1 minute more. Pour in milk and whisk to combine. Season with salt, pepper, and cayenne.

3. Bring to a boil, then reduce heat and simmer until thickened, 3 minutes. Remove from heat and pour gravy over parbaked biscuits, then top with remaining biscuits. Brush biscuits with butter and season with pepper.

4. Bake until golden and cooked through, 20 minutes.

5. Garnish with chives before serving.

LOADED CAULIFLOWER BREAKFAST BAKE

TOTAL TIME
1 HR
30 MIN

SERVES
6

We had serious doubts that cauliflower could be a formidable substitute for hash browns. But we can confidently assure you that you won't miss the potatoes.

1 large head cauliflower
8 slices bacon, chopped
10 large eggs
1 cup whole milk
2 cloves garlic, minced
2 teaspoons paprika
Kosher salt
Freshly ground black pepper
2 cups shredded cheddar
2 green onions, thinly sliced, plus more for garnish
Hot sauce, for serving

1. Preheat oven to 350°. Grate cauliflower head on a box grater and transfer to a large baking dish.

2. In a large skillet over medium heat, cook bacon until crispy, 8 minutes. Transfer to a paper towel–lined plate to drain fat.

3. In a large bowl, whisk together eggs, milk, garlic, and paprika. Season with salt and pepper.

4. Top cauliflower with cheddar, cooked bacon, and green onions, and pour over egg mixture.

5. Bake until eggs are set and top is golden, 35 to 40 minutes.

6. Garnish with hot sauce and more green onions before serving.

MORE INSANELY EASY RECIPES

You'll find everything you could possibly want in one of our cookbooks—whether it's a weeknight chicken dinner, an easy Instant Pot side, an epic air fryer appetizer, or an over-the-top dessert. **We've got it all.**

KETO FOR CARB LOVERS
100+ Amazing Low Carb, High Fat Recipes

PARTY IN AN AIR FRYER
75+ Guilt-Free Air Fryer Recipes

PARTY IN AN INSTANT POT®
75+ Crazy Simple Recipes Made in Your Multi Cooker

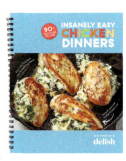

INSANELY EASY CHICKEN DINNERS
90+ Delicious Weeknight Dinners

KETO STARTER GUIDE
Essential Recipes, Tips, & Tricks For Keto Beginners

INSANE SWEETS
100+ Cookies, Bars, Bites & Treats

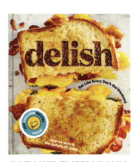

EAT LIKE EVERY DAY'S THE WEEKEND
275+ Amazing Recipe Ideas!

ULTIMATE COCKTAILS
100+ Fun & Delicious Cocktail Recipes

CHECK THEM OUT AT:
Store.Delish.com and Amazon